The Power of a Paper Clip

A Holocaust Study
in Rural Appalachia
Opens Up the World
to Its Students

Linda Hooper
Sharon Shadrick

LYSTRA BOOKS
& Literary Services

ISBN: 979-8-9877247-6-7

Library of Congress Control Number: 2024922157

Grateful acknowledgement is made to Mary Jane Higdon, Roger Payne, Bob Cusick, Josh Holtcamp, and Taylor McDaniel for permission to reprint photos from their personal collections. All other photographs are from the collections of authors Linda Hooper and Sharon Shadrick.

The authors are grateful to the interviewees whose thoughts about their participation in The Paper Clip Project helped bring this book to life.

The authors and publisher are grateful to songwriters Joe Fab ("Jubilee") and Norman Einhorn ("Beyond the Railcar") for permission to use their lyrics.

The authors and publisher have attempted to contact all of the people whose work is included in the book, much of which has not been published elsewhere. Some individuals have passed away. We were unable to contact others. If any reader has information that could allow us to include additional acknowledgements, please contact the publisher. We will be happy to make corrections in future printings.

Sharon Shadrick's back cover photo by Maygen Key Photography.

Back cover illustration by Connie Parker.

Book design by Kelly Prelipp Lojk

LYSTRA BOOKS
& Literary Services

Published by
Lystra Books & Literary Services, LLC
391 Lystra Estates Drive
Chapel Hill, NC 27517
lystrabooks@gmail.com

*This book is dedicated to the people
who made this project possible &
who are working to create
the Whitwell Education
& Heritage Center.*

CONTENTS

Introduction

When Sharon Shadrick told me about a documentary called *Paper Clips*, I was polite. Oh, I said, I'll have to watch it, thinking, a documentary about paper clips? Sure. Right away.

I met Sharon at a writing workshop in August 2023 when I gave an impromptu talk about self-publishing. I told everyone who attended, if you have more questions, email me.

Sharon had questions, and as we corresponded, I saw that she and her co-author, Linda Hooper, had a more than casual interest in publishing. They were serious about getting a book called *The Power of a Paper Clip* into print. I was intrigued.

I asked to read the first twenty pages. And I finally watched the documentary.

You may already know all about the Paper Clips Project and the movie that resulted from it. Or you may—like me, initially—have no clue why a common object sold by the hundreds at Staples deserves such dedication or attention.

The Paper Clips Project was begun by principal Linda Hooper and educators Sandra Roberts and David Smith, her colleagues at Whitwell Middle School in Whitwell, Tennessee, in 1998. Students at WMS studied the Holocaust and the effects of hatred, prejudice, and evil in the world. They taught their families and the community. They discovered that Norwegians had worn paper clips on their collars during the Nazi occupation as a symbol of resistance and solidarity with their Jewish neighbors. It was the students' idea to collect six million paper clips, one for each of the Jewish lives lost to the Holocaust.

Collecting six million paper clips turns out to be no ordinary after-school project. Cake sales and car washes won't get the job done. But the world was waiting for these kids. The world changed them, and they changed the world.

Watch *Paper Clips*. You can find it online. I recommend you have tissues at hand. Not because it is sad, but because it is as complex as human experience. It will stir a stew of emotions, and in the end, it will give you hope.

The young people of Whitwell remind us that we can make the world better. We can dissolve barriers built by fear, ignorance, and hatred. If those things reside inside us, we can be thankful that the antidotes are inside us too and are even more powerful.

The story told in this book begins before *Paper Clips* and extends past it, up to today, no matter what day it is, no matter what is happening in the world. It also offers a view of the future shaped by young people and paper clips.

The next time you see a paper clip on the sidewalk, stop and pick it up. Remember this story and slip it over your collar. You are now part of the solution.

That's the message of this story. One clip at a time.

– Nora Gaskin Esthimer
September 2024

1

The Paper Clips

The Journey
to *Paper Clips*

In the fall of 1964, Linda Hooper searched for a teaching position in the Tennessee mountains. The only opening was as a first-grade teacher at Sequatchie Elementary, a three-teacher school with grades one through six. Linda did not feel qualified for this position with her degrees in teaching high school chemistry and nutrition, but the superintendent told her, "Anybody can teach first grade."

While Linda disagreed with his sentiment, she needed a job, and the school needed a teacher. She applied, was hired for the position, and began her career with Marion County Schools. In this small rural school, Linda learned that compassion for students was as important as the subject matter she taught.

At the end of the school year, she was offered a position as coordinator of the Marion County Office of Economic Opportunity. While serving in this role, Linda observed community dynamics: "I realized how important it was for each person to have a voice in community decisions and how a lack of educational opportunities was the root of many of the problems citizens encountered."

Linda enjoyed this work, but teaching was her first love. Two years later, a teaching position opened at Whitwell High School, and she took it. However, when Linda was expecting her first child, she had to resign her teaching position. At that time a female teacher could not continue to teach if she was pregnant. She made the decision to stay home with her children until the youngest son started school.

In 1977, she resumed her career at Crossroads Elementary School, where she later became principal. She became the supervisor of instruction for Marion County Schools in 1991. Linda was ill-suited for this paperwork position, so when the position as principal at the newly created Whitwell Middle School became open, she applied and was transferred there.

It was then that all her work experience, heritage, and beliefs came together to fulfill God's plan for her.

In 1998, Linda worked with the School Improvement Council, a committee formed by Linda to encourage collaboration between parents and stakeholders of Whitwell Middle School. They determined students needed exposure to the diversity of other cultures, especially those cultures that had experienced the evils of hate and intolerance. That summer Linda asked the assistant principal, David Smith, to attend an iEARN (International Education and Resource Network) conference to learn about projects that would connect the students via the internet to students around the world.

At the conference, organizations presented projects that would encourage student growth and collaboration. David came home from the conference with the idea of teaching Whitwell Middle School students about the Holocaust. He shared his information with Principal Linda Hooper, and she began to put together a plan to make this happen. She knew two teachers who would take this challenge and run with it.

In 1998, at the project's outset, David Smith, assistant principal, and Sandra Roberts, teacher and cheer coach, agreed to lead the Holocaust study group.

David had a degree in history and had been a social studies teacher prior to becoming the assistant principal. He was also the middle school football coach and respected by the students and the community.

Teacher Sandra Roberts was asked to take the lead, teaching alongside David Smith. Sandra was a native of Whitwell and her family was involved in local church and community life. She had taught in the schools there since getting her college degree. At the time the Holocaust project was being created, she was the eighth-grade English teacher.

Sandra was also the cheer coach at Whitwell Middle School. Her classroom sparkled with Disney decorations. A Holocaust study seemed like a sharp departure from the magical environment she created for her students. But because she was deeply rooted in the community, because she was experienced at team building, and because both students and parents trusted her, she was a natural choice for the new and challenging subject.

The Holocaust intrigued her, disturbed her, confused her, and Sandra needed answers for herself as much as for her students. She agreed to take on the Holocaust study and to do so without compensation.

The Holocaust study group was not to be a fun extracurricular activity for Whitwell Middle School. The program was open to any eighth-grade student, but parental involvement was non-negotiable. The study involved delving deep into evil, evil that cost 6,000,000 Jews their lives, along with 5,000,000 non-Jewish people who openly opposed Nazis policies. The study materials were graphic in nature, and the photographs from the Holocaust were horrifying.

Children could not go into this dark abyss alone. In a small community like Whitwell where school happenings are a regular topic of discussion around town, parents needed to understand what was going on firsthand. Principal Linda Hooper required any child who wanted to attend the after-school classes to bring a parent along. If adult family members were involved, they could combat rumors that might result from this unusual after-school study.

More than anything else, the students would need their families with them on this journey, someone at home to whom they could turn when the "why" questions arose and to help them deal with the emotions this study would bring. While no adult could explain this evil, the teachers could provide comfort and question the decisions that led to this devastation of a culture. To bring awareness of the consequences of hate and intolerance, family members needed to change and grow along with the students.

In the beginning Mrs. Hooper, Mr. Smith, and Ms. Roberts were aware of the risks they took, but they were convinced the Holocaust study project was important.

During that first year of the Holocaust study group in 1998 approximately sixteen eighth-grade students and their parents began to review history, read literature, and watch documentary films about the Holocaust. They were appalled at the Nazis' inhumanity. They were heartbroken that people lost their entire families just because someone hated their religious beliefs and cultural identity. They also came to the understanding that the victims of the Holocaust were not all Jewish. Homosexuals, artists, the handicapped, and other groups were also targeted for extinction. One student in the group was from a Jehovah's Witness family. They were astonished that Jehovah's Witnesses were one of the groups that the Nazis targeted.

As the students were learning about the Holocaust, they saw similar actions that had taken place in the United States. Everyone, including Linda Hooper, was appalled to learn about the treatment of African Americans, Native Americans, and Asian Americans during World War II. Nazi Germany was not the only source of evil in the world.

As the year progressed, the students and their families realized that even the smallest of actions can lead one down a path of good or evil. Students began to soften their words to each other. Bullying dropped as the lessons students learned from this project began to be expressed in their actions.

When the year ended, parents and students of the rising eighth-grade class wanted to know if the Holocaust study group would be offered again the next year. Mrs. Hooper knew this subject had to continue as an extracurricular activity with the goal of becoming a part of the school curriculum. Thankfully, Sandra Roberts and David Smith agreed to continue to teach the class.

Linda's Background

Linda Hooper was raised in Whitwell by young, minimally educated parents. Her family was poor in material things, but rich in love and necessities. Linda didn't realize the extent of their poverty until she graduated college and had a job of her own.

Her parents valued education and supported her ambitions, but they taught her two important life lessons. First, no matter how little you had, someone always had less, and what you had must be shared. Second, to be disrespectful or cruel to another human being was to disrespect and be cruel to God because his life flame burns in all humans. These were the lessons Linda wanted her students to learn.

Whitwell, Tennessee, is a town of sixteen hundred people. It is sheltered in the Sequatchie Valley of the Appalachian Mountains. It is a community where neighbors know and care for each other. Families have lived and raised their children there for generations, teaching by example the basic values of decency, caring, and tolerance. Whitwell is a town where people want their children to have a better life and a better education than they were able to have.

Linda grew up during a time when racial segregation was the rule in this rural area of Tennessee, but Linda's dad believed race did not matter. He proved it by hosting baseball games in the field adjacent to their home where Black and white boys played baseball together with a chicken-wire backstop. Gene Westmoreland, a Black neighbor up the hill, would bring barbeque from his home-based restaurant. The families shared food and built memories, with baseball providing common ground.

As the years passed, Linda realized that these gatherings laid the foundation for her future endeavors.

Linda attended Middle Tennessee State University, earning a degree in nutrition in 1963. Her first teaching job was at White Station High School in Memphis during the 1963–64 school year. Linda's classes had a large percentage of Jewish students.

"I learned more from them than I taught them," she said in later years.

Linda and her husband, Edward, made plans to settle in western Tennessee after his graduation from pharmacy school, but Edward's father, a pharmacist in Whitwell, died. Edward and Linda returned to their hometown so he could take over the family drug store.

With these connections to the community of Whitwell, Linda was well prepared to lead the local middle school. She remembered the lessons taught by her family about reaching out to the neighbors. Except now, as she tried to introduce students and the community to a larger world, she wanted them to see their neighbors would encompass the entire world.

Six Million Paper Clips

As their study of the Holocaust progressed, the students tried to come to grips with the overwhelming numbers of people whom the Nazis murdered.

Knowledge that the Nazis kept meticulous records of the methods, times, and places of the murders, as well as how the victims' bodies were disposed of was devastating for the students of Whitwell Middle School. These young students could not comprehend the forces of evil that allowed these crimes to be committed, much less documented.

The realization that 1.5 million of these victims were children under the age of fourteen was even more heartbreaking. This tragedy now had a face for the students. These were children just like them. Yet, students from a town of sixteen hundred people could not imagine the six million Jewish exterminated souls, the total of eleven million lives lost when counting the non-Jewish victims as well.

The 2000–01 class of Holocaust study group students came to Mrs. Hooper to ask if they could collect something to visualize the six million Jewish victims.

Mrs. Hooper gave them permission with the admonition, "You can, if the objects you decide to collect are related to World War II or the Holocaust. And they must be small enough to fit in the school."

It was now up to the students to find something to represent each life lost. With no ideas in mind at that time, this thought was shelved until students could find something worthwhile.

As the Holocaust study group continued to meet and grow under Sandra Roberts's and David Smith's leadership, Whitwell Middle School's teachers also continued to grow through training. One of Mrs. Hooper's core beliefs about education is that "educators should continually search for new ideas that will make the classroom more fun, enjoyable, and interesting to their students."

In keeping with this belief, she encouraged and made it possible for staff to attend conferences relevant to their subjects. The National Middle School Conference was one of these. While at the conference in 1999, David Smith was given a brochure about teaching the Holocaust curriculum with a paper clip attached. He tossed the brochure in his bag and pulled it out later to share with the Holocaust study group taking shape. Every resource mattered.

The brochure explained the importance of the paper clip. During the Nazi occupation of their country, the Norwegian people adopted the simple, everyday object to be a symbol of resistance. To openly oppose or confront the occupiers was to risk punishment or death. Instead, Norwegians wore paper clips on their collars or lapels to show their solidarity against the Nazis.

During the discussions between Sandra Roberts, David Smith, and the students about how best to represent six million souls, David remembered the brochure from the conference and told the students about the Norwegians' act of quiet defiance.

After much study and fact checking, the Holocaust study group decided to collect paper clips with a goal of six million.

The students were excited by the discovery. They went to Mrs. Hooper for approval, and she gave it. The students were going to collect six million paper clips, one for each Jew murdered in the Holocaust.

Mrs. Hooper encouraged the students in this endeavor. It was their own idea, not one adults imposed on them. No matter what the outcome was, the experience would be meaningful. Not only were the students learning about a historical event that affected the entire world, but they were also developing skills useful in future careers.

But how were they going to do it? Collecting six million paper clips was not something they could do alone. With the help of the teachers, the students composed letters to their favorite celebrities, politicians, and anyone who might support their cause and contribute paper clips. They handwrote their letters, choosing their recipients carefully. Celebrities like Jim Carrey and Tom Bosley responded with letters, autographed pictures, and a paper clip.

While the students brainstormed ways to reach their goal of collecting six million paper clips, they continued their research as well. When they discovered the resources of the National Holocaust Museum in Washington, DC, they asked to register their project there. Mrs. Hooper had doubts that the students would amass six million paper clips, but she saw this as a good activity for building communication, planning, organizing, and geography skills. To see the students excited and involved in their learning was enough to give this effort her blessing.

Once the Paper Clips Project was officially registered on the National Holocaust Museum's website, in 1999, the public had access to the work students were doing at Whitwell Middle School. The registration was the catalyst needed to bring together an unrelated group of people and propel this project forward. It captured the attention of Lena Gitter, a ninety-plus-year-old Holocaust survivor. Lena and her husband migrated to the US before the Nazis began their plans to annihilate all Jewish people. Her husband was a physician, and she was a leader in the Montessori method of teaching children. Ms. Gitter worked with people in Mississippi during Lyndon Johnson's War on Poverty. In 1996, journalist Peter Schroeder wrote a book about her work as a Montessori teacher and an activist, and they became close friends.

When Ms. Gitter read about the non-Jewish children in the rural South trying to memorialize Holocaust victims with the collection of six million paper clips, she wanted to help. She called Peter Schroeder and his wife, Dagmar Schroeder-Hildebrand. The Schroeders were then based in Washington, DC, and covered American politics for German publications. Lena insisted that they go to Whitwell and write an article that would encourage people to make sure the students reached their goal of six million paper clips.

When the Schroeders called the school in 2000 to ask if they could come, Linda's answer was an enthusiastic "Yes!" What an opportunity for the students! Rarely did they get to meet people from outside the community, much less German newspaper correspondents.

It was exciting to think of the upcoming visit, but it was also nerve-wracking. Everyone wondered what these people would be like. The students and adults were aware of the stereotypes that exist about the American South, Southerners, and Appalachians. Would the Schroeders look at them through the prism of those stereotypes?

When the meeting took place, all those concerns were swept away. It was like the reuniting of long-lost family members. The students fell in love with the Schroeders, and the reporters fell in love with the students. It was the first of many visits between Whitwell Middle School students and this thoughtful, loving couple.

Upon their return to Washington, the Schroeders contacted their friend Dita Smith, a feature writer for the *Washington Post,* and asked her to visit Whitwell to see the work for herself.

Ms. Smith came to Whitwell expecting to find racial prejudice, remnants of the Ku Klux Klan, and other stereotypical traits she associated with the rural South. Instead, she left with a new understanding that no one deserves to be labeled because of economics, race, religion, ethnic background, or place of origin—the very lessons the Paper Clip Project was teaching.

But most importantly, the students were learning the lesson of choice: that no matter who you are, you are choosing by your actions the kind of impact you will make on the world.

Dita Smith's article "A Measure of Hope" about the Paper Clip Project appeared in the *Washington Post* during Passover on April 7, 2001.

The day it appeared, the children at Whitwell Middle School had about 150,000 paper clips. Within six weeks of the article's appearance, the school had received over 24 million paper clips and thousands of letters.

As Dita Smith said, "For generations of Whitwell eighth-graders, a paper clip will never again be just a paper clip, but instead will carry a message of patience, perseverance, empathy, and tolerance."

From an Idea to the Film
Paper Clips

On the morning the "Measure of Hope" article was published in the *Washington Post*, Rachel Pinchot was having her morning tea. When Rachel read the article about the Paper Clip Project in the *Post*, she immediately called her husband, Ari Pinchot of the Johnson Group in McLean, Virginia.

Rachel Pinchot told her husband that he must make a documentary about these students and this project.

After reading the article himself, he agreed this was a worthy topic. Mr. Pinchot contacted Mrs. Hooper by email about the possibility of his company filming a documentary of the students and their Paper Clip Project.

When she did not respond, he emailed again. And again. He began to phone Whitwell Middle School.

Mrs. Hooper told the secretaries she did not have time to speak with him.

Mrs. Hooper was very opposed to having the documentary made with good reason. In the past, the media had not been kind to this former coal mining town. A mine explosion on Whitwell Mountain killed thirteen miners on December 8, 1981. The national media reported the story and found people to interview who fit their preconceived notion that everyone in the area was violent and ignorant. Other people outside of Whitwell spoke about the community in unflattering terms.

Once, a superintendent of Marion County Schools remarked, "The further north you go in Marion County, the lower the IQ gets." Whitwell is the northernmost town in the county.

How could anyone outside of Whitwell be trusted when respect was not even given by the county's own leaders?

Besides, Linda knew these stereotypes did not reflect the true nature of the town. Though poor monetarily, the citizens of Whitwell were rich in generosity, character, and spirit. They had been wounded by the things said about them in the national media.

Outsiders had not proven themselves trustworthy, as far as Mrs. Hooper was concerned, and her students were not going to be fodder for their entertainment.

Ari Pinchot knew nothing about Mrs. Hooper's reasons for dodging him, but he was persistent. The emails continued.

His doggedness piqued Mrs. Hooper's curiosity, and she began investigating the Johnson Group. She found it was a small company made up of six people. She was impressed by what she saw. Their documentaries focused on human interest stories. Every cause they had been associated with had nothing but high praise for the group.

One morning, Mrs. Hooper arrived at school before any other staff member. When the phone rang, she answered. The man on the other end of the line introduced himself as Joe Fab of the Johnson Group. He requested that he and Ari Pinchot be allowed to come to WMS and discuss the possibility of making a documentary about the Paper Clips Project.

Perhaps the time had come. Although she still wasn't convinced this was a good idea, she agreed to let them come and present their argument. Allowing the documentary about the

Paper Clips Project to be made would give the students and the community a chance to shine and receive credit for all their hard work. It would also allow students to have a legacy to assist in continuing the project.

Mrs. Hooper arranged for Pinchot and Fab to present the proposal to the Marion County Board of Education. If the board agreed, filming would begin immediately, and as compensation, the school would receive twenty-five copies of the completed film.

What Ari Pinchot and Joe Fab did not know was that Linda had already spoken to members of the Marion County School Board about the documentary, and they were pleased with the idea. After Pinchot and Fab made their presentation, the board gave its approval to begin the filming.

Just to be sure the group understood how fiercely protective Mrs. Hooper was of the students, staff, and community, she said, "I want this documentary to be about the children. I want lots of footage of children even if they are not a part of the project. I want them to see themselves on the screen and have a sense of pride. And last, but not least, if you make these children or this community look like redneck trailer trash, I will rip your heart out and eat it for breakfast."

Filming a Documentary

With Linda Hooper's prerequisites for filming established, the film crew got busy. After completion of the film, producer Joe Fab admitted, "We were always looking for good stories but weren't sure there was enough of a story here to make a documentary. Boy, were we surprised. Much of the story happened before our eyes as we were filming."

When filmmakers Elliot Berlin and Joe Fab first came to Whitwell to film *Paper Clips,* they soon realized what a close-knit and kindhearted community the town was. Even though not everyone in the small town understood the magnitude of what was going on, they knew it had Mrs. Hooper's and the school board's approval and that was enough. They, too, trusted these filmmakers to present the town fairly and worked diligently to make this documentary happen.

Because of their intimate work with the students and the community, the filmmakers came to realize their preconceived notions about the South were not justified. These townspeople were not segregated from the rest of the world. They were knowledgeable about current events. Many were educated at the local community college or state university in Chattanooga twenty-five miles away. While their political alliances ranged from conservative to liberal, there was like-mindedness when it came to this film.

The town of Whitwell opened the doors to their homes and businesses to the filmmakers. The town was proud of their children's work and wanted to support their endeavors.

The filmmakers knew funding for this documentary was essential. Without money and distribution, it wouldn't happen. Ari Pinchot turned to a friend for help. Matthew Hiltzik was a filmmaker and head of corporate communications at Miramax. Hiltzik viewed the seven-minute pitch for the documentary and immediately went to work to bring the project to Miramax.

In respect to his Jewish heritage, Hiltzik recognized the importance of honoring and remembering the people who died. "Raising and maintaining awareness of the Holocaust inside and outside the Jewish community" was a priority for him. Hiltzik had this to say about joining this venture: "While I was still a relative film novice after two and a half years at Miramax, I had learned enough to know the power of a great story and the power of film as a medium to tell and share that story. My goal was to find a way to help support Joe Fab and his colleagues to make sure this film was made and then to do my best to ensure as many people saw it in as many places as possible. There was no real plan, and I didn't fully appreciate the effort and resources required to theatrically distribute a movie, so my expectations were open-ended, but I knew this was the perfect story to open people's eyes, to teach them and inspire them."

The German Railcar

Dita Smith's article about the Paper Clips Project had gotten Ari Pinchot's attention and response. It also brought in paper clips in numbers that overwhelmed the students at Whitwell Middle School, as well as the local post office.

By mid-2001, millions of paper clips were stored in the basement of Whitwell Middle School inside barrels that once held cleaning supplies. "How do we honor the lives these paper clips represent?" Linda Hooper asked. Those barrels located in the basement of Whitwell Middle School deserved to see the light of day.

It was suggested that the paper clips be melted into a sculpture. Mrs. Hooper could not sanction this because the clips represented lives that had been exterminated in furnaces. But better ideas were hard to come by.

The Schroeders came to Whitwell to see for themselves what they had helped to bring about. One evening at dinner with them, Mrs. Hooper said, "Wouldn't it be good if we could have an authentic German transport car to house the clips and transform it from a symbol of hate and intolerance to a symbol of hope?"

"That's it!" the Schroeders said.

From that moment on, during the filming of the documentary, the Schroeders were at work, traveling all over Germany. They

Fletcher Trucking delivers the railcar to Whitwell Middle School.

finally located an authentic transport car in a private railroad museum called Eisenbahnverein Ganzlin e.V. Robel. In the book, *Six Million Paper Clips: The Making of a Children's Holocaust Museum* (2004), the Schroeders explained that "then they saw it, and it took their breath away: Car Number 011-993, built in 1917." The car was one of only a few remaining railcars used to ship Jews to concentration and death camps. This committed couple convinced the owner of the car to sell it for the Paper Clips Project.

Next, they undertook two tasks: convincing friends and family to supply the funding and figuring out the logistics for moving the car more than 4,600 miles (about 7,400 km) by rail and sea. The German national railway agreed to transport the car to the port of Cuxhaven. Once at the German port, the Schroeders were able to use their influence to have the car transported on a Norwegian ship, *The Blue Sky,* to the port of Baltimore.

The ship arrived in Baltimore in late August 2001. Before it could be offloaded, it had to be inspected and disinfected. It was ironic that a German tank was also aboard *The Blue Sky.* When the ship's hull was opened, the tank's gun turret pointed directly at the railcar. Elliot Berlin, a member of the *Paper Clips* film crew was there and observed, "No matter what happened in the past, this car was able to overcome a Nazi assault."

The railcar was en route to Whitwell when the 9/11 attack occurred in New York City. The country was in shock over the thousands of lives lost due to airline hijackings and planes being flown into the twin towers and Pentagon by al-Qaeda Islamic extremists. This historic event highlighted the need to educate people about the difference between intolerance and hate.

Everyone involved with the project realized the difference between the impulse behind *Paper Clips* and the 9/11 attack. *Paper Clips* would show to the world that a loving, dedicated group can overcome any obstacle. The German railcar would send a message to the world that all lives are important. In a world where all lives are valued, the horrors of what happened in that railcar could not happen again. Commercial aircraft full of innocent people would not become weapons of war.

The Teamsters Union in Baltimore loaded the car onto a train provided by CSX Transportation. The train transported the car to Chattanooga, where B&B Crane Co. loaded it onto a truck provided by Fletcher Trucking to bring it to its final destination.

When the car arrived in Whitwell, it was set on tracks provided by CSX. Hash marks and numbers stamped on the tracks show they were made during the months of September and October of 1941.

The Roberts, Higdon, and Powell families of Whitwell worked diligently to create a lovely park around the car. Linda Pickett, a local artist, designed a butterfly sculpture to be placed

Kevin Higdon directing work on the railcar.

alongside the car, as well as stepping stones decorated with painted butterflies. Later these painted butterflies were covered in stained glass by local artist Jacky Lofty. These art pieces were designed to honor the children who perished at the Terezin Concentration Camp.

The railcar and its setting were designated the Children's Holocaust Memorial.

There had been no fancy fundraising campaigns. Social media did not exist. Everything needed for the Children's Holocaust Memorial was contributed by individuals or businesses who heard about the project through word of mouth, letters, or an internet search. Everything from the paper clips collected to the memorial itself was a result of individual and grassroots efforts.

Students, educators, and community members all acknowledged that a far higher power was involved in making this project a success and in garnering the attention of the world. There was a realization that this project was an accomplishment far beyond any human endeavor.

The Roberts family works on landscaping at the memorial site.

Linda Hooper explained, "As the car was set in place on the tracks, I was overwhelmed by powerful emotions. Looking at the students, parents, teachers, and community, I reflected on the journey that had brought us to this day. As the giant crane lifted the car and set it on the tracks, I was struck by the tremendous responsibility that our community had accepted. We would transform this symbol of death and hate to one of life and hope. At that moment it was as if I had been transported to another place. My mind knew I was at Whitwell Middle School, but my emotions were suddenly overwhelmed by giant spotlights, screams, menacing dogs barking, and harsh commands. I could see Nazi soldiers forcing people from the car. I could feel the confusion of people leaving the car. Their fear smothered me like a hot, wet blanket. And over it all hung a sky dusted with ashes and the smell of burning flesh. I wanted to run and hide. But that was not to be. One of our Holocaust students said, 'Mrs. Hooper, you need to go into the car.'

"Inside the car I could feel the spirits of victims who had traveled to the camps. Even though I was alone in the nine feet by twenty-five feet space, my body felt compressed, my breathing labored as if I were sharing the air with a hundred other souls. I saw two holes in the floor and two in the ceiling, a reminder that this car transported grain before the war. There were no windows. At that moment, I was convinced if the doors to the car closed, I would die from fear.

"I have no idea how long I was in the car. Finally, two of the students who had worked so hard, Casey Condra and Cassie Crabtree, came into the car looking for me. They must have seen I was distressed because they embraced me. Outside I could hear the voices of all the people who were working to create this memorial. I lifted a prayer for all the victims of Nazi hatred. And I thanked God for all those who had made this memorial possible."

A Community Steps Up

As the documentary team began its work in Whitwell, its employees needed to be fed, housed, and entertained.

No fancy hotels or restaurants were available to accommodate them, so people like Mary Jane and Kevin Higdon answered Linda Hooper's call for help. Both Mary Jane and Kevin grew up in Whitwell. With two sons, Gregory and Jonathan, enrolled in Whitwell schools, the Higdons were already active in their children's education. Both boys participated in the Holocaust study group.

This family assumed responsibility, even though to do so required a shy country boy like Kevin Higdon to talk and socialize with people outside his comfort zone. Mary Jane remodeled her home (unbeknownst to Linda) to entertain out-of-town strangers as guests.

The Higdons' involvement started out like that of most parents at Whitwell Middle School. They helped with student activities in the Holocaust study group. Mary Jane counted paper clips and took hundreds of pictures to fill scrapbooks for documentation. Kevin put his family construction business work on hold as he and his father's construction crew built the platform for the railcar.

Somewhere along the line, this Whitwell family became so invested in the project, it became their life. When Kevin hammered nails into the roof of the railcar to repair it, he felt like he was "hurting someone." He didn't want to leave it alone and felt he should "stay with it."

They may not have been able to reach into the past to help the Jewish people then, but they were part of the community that provided a place for the Jewish people to grieve and honor their lost families in the present and future.

While their political opinions and religion may have differed, the Higdons and their visitors found kinship through the project. When politics worked its way into discussions, Mary Jane explained, "I can disagree with someone and still be friends."

Holocaust Survivors Visit Whitwell

In 2001, four Holocaust survivors made the trip to Whitwell. Bernard Igielski, Rachel Gleitman, Joe Grabczak, and Sam Sitko shared their experiences of suffering and eventual freedom.

The small United Methodist Church was within walking distance of Whitwell Middle School, and its wooden pews were packed with Whitwell townspeople. Parents, families, and students had been prepared by the Holocaust study group for this event, but meeting the survivors, hearing the stories, and seeing the marks of their captivity firsthand removed barriers that separated book knowledge from reality.

Bernard Igielski spent ten days in a railcar on his way to a concentration camp in Germany when he was a young boy. In the camp, he and his friends made a game of capturing and counting lice and trying to guess who had the most.

Rachel talked about walking into a gas chamber disguised as a bathhouse with her mother, sister, and aunts, whom she told, "No water is going to come out of those showers." Thankfully, the gas chamber malfunctioned, and they were set free to return to the barracks.

At the close of the event, the line to shake the victims' hands was long. Hearts were overwhelmed by the stories told. The people of Whitwell embraced each of the survivors, showing appreciation for their lives and the impact their stories had on the community.

Dedication & Butterflies

While the dedication of the railcar was a moment of satisfaction for the students of Whitwell Middle School, for the Holocaust survivors and their families it was even more. More than just a memorial for those who were lost during Hitler's reign, more than just a railcar to house paper clips, it was a celebration of hope. Although multitudes of their kinsmen had been destroyed, their people and culture lived on. Scarred, yet determined to educate and tell their stories, they spoke, following the admonition of those killed: "Remember and tell."

On a summer-like day on November 9, 2001, the bleachers (lent by the Marion County Fair) outside the railcar were filled. People flew in from cities across the US and even other countries to celebrate this moment. Jewish families came to celebrate the creation of a place to honor their deceased loved ones. Joe Fab, Elliott Berlin, Bob Johnson, and Matthew Hiltzik were there. The town of Whitwell was there.

They may have come together for different reasons, but with a single purpose: the dedication of the Children's Holocaust Memorial.

Roger Payne, music educator at Whitwell Middle School, prepared the chorus to perform an original song written by Ellen Hubert and Sharon Lands Shepherd. Payne said, "They had sent a handwritten manuscript of the song 'We Shall Not Forget'

The railcar houses 11,000,000 paper clips—6,000,00 representing the Jewish people killed during the Holocaust and 5,000,000 for the deaths of other persecuted groups.

to Linda and asked that we sing it sometime. Linda brought it to me and suggested that we sing it at the railcar dedication. Because it was handwritten, it was a little hard to read. I looked at Linda and said, 'I'm not sure I can read this,' to which she replied, 'Sure you can.' So, I figured it out, and the chorus was outstanding at the performance. The haunting melody and lyrics really get your soul."

One of the speakers at the dedication was Martha Rich, a survivor of Auschwitz. Martha and Linda Hooper immediately connected when they met for the first time that day. Barbara Wind, a friend of Martha Rich, wrote about their unique friendship saying, "Both are women of spirit, charm, and steely determination."

Martha bravely spoke of not allowing the Nazis to take her spirit away. During her speech, a flock of yellow butterflies flitted between the attendees and the railcar as if to remind them: This is not the ghetto; butterflies do live here! And like butterflies, we can all overcome a dark, enclosed space to emerge with a beauty of spirit that will inspire the whole world. The Children's Holocaust Memorial celebrated the survival of a people without forgetting those who were lost.

The Screening of
Paper Clips in Whitwell

"*As we reflect on the journey we have made, we are humbled and amazed at the impact our community, our faculty, and our students have had on the world. My thoughts
go back to 2001 and the dedication of the Children's Holocaust Memorial. The spirit of love, tolerance, and goodwill
that was present there was simply overwhelming. To see
the faces of the people who made this memorial, to think
of the love and labor they represent, to hear the school
chorus sing the butterfly song is to realize that dedication
and hard work can overcome any obstacles. Now, here we
are. The documentary will be presented to the students, the
community, and the world, giving a lesson in tolerance, respect, and love.*"

– **Linda Hooper**, principal of
Whitwell Middle School

On November 8, 2003, the public was invited to view the
documentary movie about how an idea to add diversity to
Whitwell Middle School's curriculum led to the creation of the
Children's Holocaust Memorial in the railcar. *Paper Clips* didn't

Whitwell Middle School announces the November 8, 2003, premiere of the Paper Clips *documentary. Tickets were $5, with proceeds going toward a scholarship fund for WMS students.*

At left: Matthew Hiltzik, left, with students Casey Condra and Amber Webb. At right: Linda Hooper welcomes visitors to the Paper Clips *premiere at Whitwell Middle School.*

open at a fancy theater with red carpet; it was screened in the small Whitwell Middle School auditorium. The tickets were five dollars each, with proceeds going toward a scholarship fund for WHS students who graduated that year.

People who had worked on the film in different capacities were brought together, some for the first time. When Linda met Matthew Hiltzik in person after many phone conversations, she was surprised. "He is much younger than I expected for someone who is so successful."

Matthew's first impression of Linda was the same as he has of her today: "[She is] intelligent, proud, committed, charismatic, creative, engaging, protective, and firm, while managing to be warm and nurturing at the same time. You had to earn her trust, but she was willing to give you a fair shot."

Before the screening, Linda and her husband, Edward, wanted Matthew to see the beauty of the area, so they drove him up to the mountain for a view of the Sequatchie Valley.

From Matthew's perspective, Whitwell reminded him of "some smaller towns in upstate New York that I was used to seeing during my travels as press secretary for the New York State Democratic Party. It felt a little bit like you were passing through a movie set, where you knew there was some real life and activity, but it was clearly muted from what had been there in the past—there was small-town charm but some clear challenges. It made sense when I later learned about Whitwell's history of the mine closing and the decimated local economy, but I knew from my previous experience that even though times may have been tough and jobs were moving away, the people in town were just as committed as ever to their children."

Joe Fab and Julia Eddy, the two people who spent long hours editing the film, arrived. Joe was also the person who spent the most time in Whitwell supervising the filming of *Paper Clips*. Joe's wife Kay accompanied him. Bob Johnson, who had gambled on having his company make the film, came.

Grammy Award-winning singer Alison Kraus sang the theme song "Jubilee" for the documentary, and she came to the premiere. Linda recalled, "Everyone wanted Alison's autograph and to have a picture made with her. She was more than gracious and accommodating."

Cheryl White and Andrae Zohn, who sang with Alison on the soundtrack, accompanied her. Alison brought Sam, her four-year-old son, and Cheryl brought her daughter, Rachel. Linda was "gratified to have so many of the people featured in the film and those who brought it to life attend the premiere." The events surrounding the premiere were like a huge family reunion.

Jubilee
(Arranged by Charlie Burnett and Joe Fab)

The sun came up on Monday morn,
The world was all in flames
It's all a mortal man can do
To make it right again
Swing and turn, Jubilee
Live and learn, Jubilee

The moon came up, I stood my ground
And swore to not give in,
To never rest and do my best
To rid this world of sin.
Swing and turn, Jubilee
Live and learn, Jubilee.

The one who spoke cried tears of hope
That we might change in time,
And when I looked into her eyes
The fear I saw was mine.

Swing and turn, Jubilee
Live and learn, Jubilee.

The time had come to travel on
I made my way alone
My soul will mend at Journey's end
The road will take me home.
Swing and turn, Jubilee
Live and learn, Jubilee.

Linda had already seen the movie at Bob Johnson's home, and she was anxious about how the local community would receive the film. She explained, "My anxiety was short-lived at the pre-

miere, overcome by the powerful message of the documentary. As the film concluded, there was silence. The audience was overcome with pride in the students, but that was tempered with shock and sadness at

Some of the people who made the film possible— Julia Edy, Joe Fab, the Schroeders, Matthew Hiltzik, and Bob Johnson— along with a group of WMS students after the showing of Paper Clips.

WMS students Jonathan Higdon, Robbyn Reynolds, Chris Johnson, Breezy Hudson, Molly Bailey, Steven Austin, and Holly Perkins from the 1999–2000 school year Holocaust study group at the Paper Clips *premiere.*

the images of the victims. The scene where the car is traveling to Whitwell on September 11 as the terrorist attack is taking place in New York brought an awareness of just how important the work of our students is in combating evil. It was as if the audience was filled with too many emotions to express. Then suddenly an emotional tsunami rolled through the auditorium. People hugged and smiled at each other. It was uplifting to hear the positive comments and receive hugs of gratitude from the audience as they exited the auditorium."

"I knew that distributing this film would put Whitwell on the map as a real destination for visitors around the world,"

At left: Edward Hooper, Linda Hooper, and Alison Krauss at the premiere. At right: Mary Jane Higdon with Alison Krauss.

Hiltzik said. "Not only that, but the trajectory of people's lives would be changed by being a part of this film."

On the morning after the screening, Matthew experienced "one of the most powerful moments of my life when I said my morning prayers in the railcar. There was this heightened level of spirituality and a feeling that in some way I had successfully carried on the tradition of the Jewish people by being able to pray to and thank God in this railcar, which had carried my people to their deaths ... that thanks to the people of Whitwell, I had a chance to have a moment that proved love and faith and good hearted, wise people coming together to celebrate the values we share will defeat hate every time."

Despite Linda Hooper's initial trepidation about the making of the film, the final product exceeded all her expectations. The town of Whitwell was portrayed realistically, and the film preserved its Appalachian dignity. Poverty was not hidden, but the spotlight shone on the work accomplished in spite of it. The filmmakers had successfully created a film that treated the townspeople and its children with respect and honor.

2

Local to Global

Positive Letters

As the Paper Clips Project became known for its work in teaching tolerance and diversity, letters and emails began to arrive, as did visitors. For the Jewish community the railcar was a place to grieve loved ones by placing paper clips inside the memorial instead of flowers on a grave.

Although the project goals were met and exceeded, the power of the project and documentary was echoed with every click of an email or letter addressed to the Children's Holocaust Memorial in Whitwell, Tennessee. One letter read, "We never had a place to pray for their souls that we felt was meaningful until I visited your Holocaust Memorial."

With this encouragement, Whitwell Middle School was tasked by the world to keep going. One supporter wrote: "I am the child of survivors of the Holocaust.… I am enclosing ten paper clips for your collection to represent only those members of our immediate family who perished in the Holocaust. This, of course, does not include extended family members, nor does it include the many unborn generations, which no longer have any chance of being born."

Another letter from a child of a Holocaust survivor said, "It is only by the grace of G-d that my father survived and that I am alive today. I am enclosing eight paper clips for your collection.

Teach your students that we must <u>NEVER</u> forget the lessons of racism and genocide."

Stories of survivors made their way to Whitwell. One survivor, Bernard Storch, escaped the Nazis and went on to join the Polish army as a frontline soldier. He told this story in a letter mailed to the school: "You can't possibly imagine the devastating impact it has on a frontline soldier upon entering factory-like buildings and discovering that the facility was a Death Camp where innocent men, women, and children from all over Europe lost their lives.... Before I entered that facility, I had no knowledge of extermination camps and many things ran thru my mind. *To this day this picture is in front of my eyes.*

"My father's two remaining brothers were in a refugee camp, which was too full up to allow him in. He managed to enter the camp by taking on the identity of someone inside who died. In 1948 he left his brothers to come to the United States. I remain with that dead man's last name."

One story of survival mirrored Anne Frank's. "My mother survived with her parents by being hidden by a gentile family for two and a half years, much like Anne Frank was (fortunately with a happier ending)."

One Australian student wrote about being devastated over the "suffering and torment [the Jewish people] endured." She was also shocked by her classmates' reactions and "amazed at how hard-hearted they were."

Linda Hooper wrote back with these encouraging words: "Know that creating an atmosphere of tolerance, acceptance, respect, and love for our fellow man is a difficult task. Every year when school begins, I ask God to just help me to know that I have made a positive difference in one life. We cannot change things overnight. We must look around us and find one other person who wants to change and that we can relate to. That is how change begins. One person at a time."

The Policeman

"As long as there is hatred and prejudice in this world, we all have a responsibility to work together to end it."

–Andrew Perkel

One letter that especially resonated with Linda came from a police officer in Austin, Texas. Andrew Perkel had wanted to be a police officer since he was five years old, and with good reason.

Andrew grew up in a middle-class neighborhood in Philadelphia. As a child, he lived a tormented life because of a bully, Roy, who lived down the street. Roy took pleasure in blackening Andrew's eyes in second grade and telling him to stay away from his brothers.

Andrew was puzzled by this hatred from a kid only a year older than himself. What had he done to make him so mad? It would be ten years before Andrew would get answers—ten years of bullying in the meantime.

After all that time, one day while the boys rode home on the school bus, Roy said to Andrew, "Why don't you take all your Jewish friends and go back to Israel?"

There it was. In that one statement, Andrew realized what all the torment had been about: anti-Semitism.

Andrew had not done anything to Roy to make him mad. When Roy punched him in the face as he was walking away,

Andrew had an epiphany. He realized there would be no end to his treatment unless he decided to do something about it. Andrew made the decision to start lifting weights and get strong enough to defend himself.

He sent a message through a mutual friend that if Roy came near him again, he would regret it. With Andrew's newfound strength and determination, Roy left him alone.

Dealing with anti-Semitism from a young age gave Andrew insight and wisdom about himself as well. He said in the letter, "In spite of Roy, I have always tried to respond to anti-Semitism with understanding and an attempt to educate those I come in contact with. Fortunately, I realized that if I simply beat up those who made anti-Semitic remarks, not only would I give someone a reason to hate Jews, I was then no better than Roy." Instead of a negative path of revenge, Andrew chose to become a police officer.

When Andrew saw *Paper Clips*, he was moved by the love and acceptance from the small-town children who, unlike Roy, offered hope, understanding, and friendship. His letter went on to say, "Your project has given me a sense of peace and protection from many 'Roys' in this world. What I mean is, I can spend the rest of my life trying to protect myself and others from harm generated by ignorant hatred and never scratch the surface of those who suffer at the hands of the bullies in this world ... For any bully who might see the film, it hopefully will make them stop and think about how wrong and hurtful they are when they attack with blind prejudice."

The ultimate message from Andrew's final paragraph touched Linda the most. He wrote, "As long as there is hatred and prejudice in this world, we all have a responsibility to work together to end it. I felt it was important to tell you that you and your students have accomplished something in one project that most of us would hope to accomplish in our lifetime and our children's lifetime."

Negative Letters

As articles, television reports, and the documentary itself brought more attention to the Paper Clips Project, not all reactions were positive. With over thirty thousand positive letters received, the fewer than two hundred negative letters pale in comparison. Negative letters and emails came from a diverse group of people. Surprisingly, some of the criticism came from Jews and academics who interpreted history differently.

According to one letter, "Organized Jewry has a BIG vested interest in keeping the lie alive." The lie being the number of Jews killed in the Holocaust. The letter continues "It was shown that no evidence existed to prove the Germans deliberately killed inmates at any camp in Germany."

One such email stated: "[WMS students] will now be more prone than ever to mix with non-whites, have gay friends, and minimize their European history in favor of Third World-ism."

One letter contained a straightened paper clip with the statement, "I enclose a straightened-out clip for your school's paper clip project. Perhaps it might help straighten out your own twisted thinking. HITLER WAS RIGHT."

Another letter contains the admonition, "You should be ashamed of yourself. The paper clips you are receiving should represent the six million lies the Jews have been pushing out since WWII."

Some letters accused the Jewish people of being "in command of most all nationwide entertainment propaganda and the news media." One claimed that the "Holocaust is the money-making machine that enriched American Jewish organizations, vastly increasing their political power and influence."

One letter criticized the school's choice to teach diversity through the project because " [the Jewish people] betrayed Jesus Christ when they crucified him on the cross." Another hand-written letter said, "Ignorance does not get any worse than your paper clip. May God have mercy on your souls."

Students read these letters and carefully placed them in a binder on the shelves of the Children's Holocaust Memorial to preserve history in the making.

When asked about the school's response to these letters, Linda Hooper said, "We have never responded to the negative letters. Think about people who constantly insult or bully other people. Everybody knows a bully. [WMS students] are not going to change those people by responding to them in a negative way or trying to point out something. What you have to do is let your actions lead the way. You must always stay focused and on the path to change the world. One clip, one act at a time."

The Two Visitors

Whitwell Middle School moved into a new building in 2008, but before that move, the Children's Holocaust Memorial Railcar remained situated directly in front of the old school building, easily catching the eye of any out-of-town visitor. During the school year, students gave tours, and the campus was a lively place. You might see students picking up trash around the campus, attending sports practices, or engaged in fundraising projects for local organizations.

However, during the month of July, the weather is unbelievably hot and humid, almost like being covered in a boiled, wet, wool blanket. July is the month Linda Hooper liked best as principal. Summer school was over. The demands of beginning a new school year were not quite pressing. This quiet month gave her time to reflect on the past year and think about the strengths and weaknesses of the school programs and her own professional needs.

Several years after the documentary was filmed, around 2006, Linda was in the old WMS building. Everything was quiet, and the doors and windows were open. Her back was to the office door as she worked in peace and concentration. Soon, she realized she wasn't alone and turned to see an elderly couple standing in the doorway.

"May I help you?" she asked.

With heavy Israeli accents, they told their story. They had flown across the country and then drove almost three hours to visit the Children's Holocaust Memorial. They looked frail and exhausted. It was hard for Linda not to cry as they shared the details of their journey. Although weary, the determination and desire to be there radiated from both of them. "We came to see the boxcar. We have brought something to place in the car."

"May I get you something? Maybe a glass of water?" Linda offered.

"No, we just want to go to the car." This married couple had a mission, and they were fixed on completing it.

As they walked toward the railcar, they began to share their memories with Linda. Like most children, they told their story in fragments, occasionally talking over each other in their rush to share.

They told Linda they had known each other since childhood. They grew up in the same neighborhood and went to school together. They practiced music, played games, and celebrated Shabbat. Their families were neighbors. Life was secure. Family taught them, loved them, protected them. Before the Holocaust, their childhood was carefree and they were surrounded by close, loving families.

Then the persecutions began. "Dirty Jew! Christ killer!" people said. Non-Jewish friends turned away from them at school, in the classroom, and on the playground. Signs appeared in store windows. "Jews not welcome." Newspaper articles portrayed Jews as the cause of all economic woes in Europe. Cartoons depicted Jews as monsters with huge noses drinking the blood of babies. Even though Linda had heard similar stories, it didn't lessen the shock of being told firsthand by survivors of the atrocities.

The Jewish couple reminisced about this time period aloud. Still to that day they could not comprehend this hatred that had been growing toward them. They had been children. They had not hurt anyone. The people who were turning away from them and insulting them were people who had shared their food, with whom they had played. Former friends were throwing rocks at them and chasing them down the street shouting the dirtiest epithets. Security was a thing of the past. Going out in the streets was not safe. A person would leave home for work or go to the grocery and disappear. Fear was suffocating all the joy from their lives. Then Jewish families were told they could only live in one area of their city. The man explained, "The authorities assured us this was for our safety. Take only what you can carry for now, we were told."

Thus began their life in a ghetto. Both their families ended up in the same place. Each family crammed into a one-room apartment. Food was scarce. A whole fresh potato was considered a blessing that could become soup to be shared by an entire family. Freezing temperatures inside the apartment in winter gave way to oppressive heat in summer. Starvation was a hungry animal lurking outside the door every day. Only the sacrifice and ingenuity of their parents provided enough food to maintain their lives.

One day the streets were filled with Nazi soldiers. Loud-speakers blared, "Everyone out of the building." As they came out into the street, they clung to the hands of their parents. Soldiers surrounded them. They began to herd them toward the rail station. People were pushing, shoving, trying to hold on to loved ones. Both of them lost their parents. Along with so many others, they found themselves at the open doors of a cattle car. Soldiers threw the Jewish people into the car if they were too slow or too small to climb in without help. When the car was packed with bodies, the door slammed shut. Friends and neigh-bors were crammed so tightly that even moving a hand was im-possible. The car began to move. Bodies bumped and swayed against the others in the car. The sounds of crying, the sounds of the train, the sounds of breathing filled the car, and sucked all sense of security from them. They do not know how long they were in the car. They only knew that when it stopped, bright lights were focused on them. The platform was covered with snarling dogs and armed soldiers.

Families were separated and sent to a living hell. The next years were filled with awful memories that the couple still did not talk about. What they did talk about was the miracle that they endured the horrors. They were able to find some surviv-ing friends and family members after the war and were blessed to come to the United States.

The woman spoke, "We married and have had a wonder-ful life here. But, my mama and papa, my husband's mama and papa were murdered by the Nazis. We do not know where their bodies were buried. Every night we go to sleep with no peace wondering where they are."

The woman took a tiny homemade envelope out of her purse. "In this envelope we put four paper clips, one for each of them. When we put them in your car, we will be able to think of them surrounded by children who love and respect them. This will bring us peace."

Linda and the couple continued to walk together to the car. As they stepped inside, the husband opened the glass door housing all the other paper clips. With tenderness and love they placed the envelope on top of the other clips. Stepping back, they embraced and breathed a sigh of relief.

Looking back on this memory, Linda said, "To have the priv-ilege of being here with this couple as they found a resting place for their pain, and to at last know where the spirits of their parents are and will be honored … if we never accomplish anything else with this project, this moment is enough."

South Africa:
Education Is the Key

As *Paper Clips* gained attention on an international level, more opportunities became available for students in this rural town. Sometimes, people showed up without fanfare or appointments. Touched deep in their soul by the work done here, they wanted to meet with the faculty of Whitwell Middle School who made this project possible.

On most school mornings, Linda arrived before the rest of the school staff with the exception of the custodians. She liked to get there early to begin her day with few interruptions before the stresses of being a middle school principal began.

One morning in 2006, a car pulled into the parking lot and four people emerged, catching her as she entered the front door.

"Good morning," they called out. Janice B. Levy, Isaac Hasson and his wife, and Darryle Fine were South African citizens. They had learned of the project and had come not only to see the work of WMS students but to propose a collaboration, one that would lead Linda to take Jenny Frazier, a former Paper Clips Project member, to South Africa to begin a student exchange between the students of Cape Town and Whitwell.

The trip was Jenny Frazier's first experience out of the country, and she was nervous about leaving her family and America behind. Since this was just a few years post 9/11, fears of hijackings and violence were uppermost in her sixteen-year-old mind.

In addition to those worries, Jenny had been warned by the people in her community about the history of apartheid in South Africa and the effects on the population. With her study of the Holocaust and the devastation it wrought on the Jewish people and others who were different, she was uncertain how this visit would go. It seemed blatant discrimination and disparity would be in the forefront.

After arriving in Cape Town, Linda and Jenny were embraced by Janice B. Levy, Darryl Fine, the Hassons, and the Cohens—the people who would go on to create the Foundation for Tolerance and Cultural Diversity.

Linda and Jenny spent the first day or two in a lovely bubble of comfort and hospitality. They visited schools whose students had viewed *Paper Clips*. They were safe within their comfort zone.

However, the tour planned for the township of Langa the next day ripped away the illusion of normalcy and revealed the impoverished side of Cape Town just a few miles from where they had been so warmly welcomed.

Linda explained, "My first sight of the Langa township made me think of a circus tent that had been burned, leaving only a skeletal frame. I later learned that this skeleton contained electrical cables for families who could afford power. Tiny concrete houses were scattered among open toilet areas. People were cooking whole animals that I could not identify over fires burning in huge metal drums. The entire area was a maelstrom of constantly moving humanity. Cardboard boxes and sheets of roofing tin formed living quarters for many. Nothing had prepared me for the poverty I was viewing."

For Jenny Frazier, the lessons learned from the Paper Clips Project would be tested. Jenny shared this moment in the *South Pittsburg Hustler*, "Thursday, we went to what was known as the Townships. These consisted of hundreds of thousands of little tin houses in which whole families live. I couldn't even bear to take pictures. I had been fitted with a microphone for the camera crew filming us, and I knew the sound guy could hear my sobs. I couldn't believe that people were actually living this way. And what made me angrier still was that there were guided tours of these poor people's villages. I know it was so those who came would send money to help, but my mind was so irrational at that moment, I was mad at the world for letting this happen."

As Linda and Jenny toured through the township in the comfortable car provided by their hosts, a sense of voyeurism troubled them both. Linda described her feelings: "How can I sit in this vehicle and stare at the horrible conditions under which thousands of people are living? What right do I have to be here, overfed, warmly dressed, and chauffeured around in this comfortable car while these people do not have running water, toilets, medical care, or even enough to eat?"

However, even in this place with the nauseating smells and garbage everywhere, there was hope. Hope took the form of a huge transport container being used as a school. Linda observed the children coming out. "The school had no windows, no air conditioning, no educational tools, just paper, pencil, crayons, and a few books. Yet, the children are sparkling clean, their faces eager. Their desire to learn hits you like a powerful jolt of electricity."

Led by their teacher, the children sang songs praising God, and behind them was a brightly painted block building with the slogan: EDUCATION IS THE KEY. Linda explained, "Although these educators and the church that sponsors this school cannot fix everything wrong here, they do not make excuses. They just do the best with what they have to make things better one child at a time."

When Linda and Jenny left the school, they went to a two-room block building called Rosie's Kitchen. In this small space, Rosie prepared lentil soup for the children of Langa. Each day Rosie fired up her propane heaters and prepared huge pots of soup. The children lined up with their plastic bowls for possibly their only meal of the day. While their mamas work in the city for affluent families, Rosie feeds the children.

Jenny and Linda were there to dip soup into the bowls and wash dishes under a cold-water faucet. With no hot water available, no basic sanitation, and no adults to wipe noses, Rosie served food amid crushing poverty, smiling, encouraging the children, nourishing not only their bodies, but their souls.

After a visit to Robben Island and a look at Nelson Mandela's prison cell, Linda said, "To stand in Mandela's cell and visualize his tall frame in that tiny space for twenty years was to be awed that this man had the courage and forgiveness not to give in to bitterness nor seek revenge. My thoughts went back to the mistreatment of our American Indians, the struggle of African Americans during the Civil Rights era, and our treatment of Japanese Americans during World War II. What kind of person would I be if I had to endure the indignities that these people suffered in their struggle for equality and human rights? Would I have a spirit of forgiveness?"

After visiting the affluent sections of Cape Town, the ghettos of Langa, Rosie's Kitchen, Nelson Mandela's cell, and an orphanage caring for children with AIDS, Linda and Jenny struggled with what they had experienced. The problems were so vast, but the Foundation for Tolerance and Cultural Diversity was using its influence to bring awareness to the needs of these poverty-stricken people, to improve access to education and to seek solutions for the problems. According to Linda, "No group can solve all of any society's problems, but using the power of one, a positive difference can be made. Then it struck me, the Paper Clips Project is like this. A group of students, a community with few resources, and no political power is teaching the world that everyone can contribute to make a positive change in our world."

Janice B. Levy, the Hassons, and Darryl Fine were also instrumental in planning Gregory Higdon and Chris Echemendia's trip to Cape Town, South Africa, as a reward for their participation in the Holocaust study group.

Although it wasn't easy for Kevin and Mary Jane Higdon to send their son on a twenty-hour plane trip, they knew it would be a lifetime experience he wouldn't forget. Sitting in Nelson Mandela's chair in a jail cell in South Africa changes a person. Touring areas of abject poverty in Cape Town with armed guards changes a person. Meeting a Nobel Prize winning peacekeeper changes a person—and a family.

Consequently, because they were there at the right place at the right time, another opportunity came their way. Gregory Higdon explained, "When we got back to the States, we went to Washington, DC, to interview Archbishop Desmond Tutu. He was incredibly kind and loved hearing stories of the Paper Clips Project. He also made sure we understood the importance of what we, as a community, were doing. It's something I'll never forget."

For Janice B. Levy, Greg Higdon and Jenny Frazier became like her own children.

Alan "Ace" Greenberg, chairman of Bear Stearns, was a supporter of the Paper Clips Project and established a scholarship fund for students. He honored Linda by naming it the Hooper

Chris Echemendia, Archbishop Desmond Tutu, and Gregory Higdon meet in Washington, DC.

Scholarship. After Gregory graduated from high school, the scholarship helped him attend the University of Tennessee at Knoxville and earn a degree in supply chain management.

Reflecting on the changes in his life directly related to the Paper Clips Project, Gregory said, "I don't have the words to do justice to the effect the project has had on my life. If I had to sum it up, I'd say that though the Sequatchie Valley was a beautiful place to grow up, there's so much outside of the land between Whitwell and Suck Creek mountains. [The Holocaust] showed me what the world can be without empathy. We're all different (religiously, socioeconomically, politically, etc.). But, if any person is being shown injustice, it's the responsibility of us all to stand up. There are no lines that should separate us from showing empathy towards one another."

Solomon Schechter Day School and Whitwell Middle School Students

When Linda Hooper visited Boston in early 2006 for the screening of the documentary *Paper Clips*, she met David Ganz, one of the main supporters of the Solomon Schechter Day School. The Solomon Schechter Day School is a private school where the Jewish religion is the foundation of their education. During their meeting, Ganz told Linda about a project his school had undertaken. As students from Whitwell Middle School were collecting paper clips to honor those killed in the Holocaust, students from Solomon Schechter Day School were collecting memories from survivors on audio. The schools chose two different avenues, but each had a heart for the same result: To raise awareness about tolerance and peace by remembering the Holocaust.

For the Schechter students, this remembrance took the form of interviews. According to *The Patriot Ledger*, "Jane Taubenfield Cohen, Schechter principal, drew on the childhood lessons of her father, a Holocaust survivor, to begin the school's L'Chaim Project in 2001. L'chaim is a Jewish toast that means 'to life' in Hebrew. The students contacted Holocaust survivors

Roger Payne and Sarah Dunn directing the joint Solomon Schechter Day School and Whitwell Middle School choirs.

around the Boston area to interview them about their experiences and record them on audio CDs."

Ganz and Hooper knew this connection between their students could not be ignored or neglected. They must bring them together. So, on January 27, Holocaust Memorial Day, Hooper returned to Boston with a small group of Whitwell Middle School students to visit the school. During this visit, the student choir from Solomon Schechter sang traditional Yiddish and Hebrew songs. Linda was so moved by their presentation that she wanted her students to learn the songs as well.

When she first presented the idea to both WMS choir director Roger Payne and his students, the initial reaction from all was, "You expect us to learn to sing in Hebrew and Yiddish? You expect us to join with a group of Jewish students and sing in Hebrew and Yiddish before an audience? You expect us to be prepared to do this in a month? Do you know that none of us speak any foreign language, much less Hebrew or Yiddish?"

Linda's answer was, "Not only do I expect you to do this, but I know you will give a perfect performance."

So, practice, they did. In March 2006, twenty-one students would visit the Schechter School to perform in a choir composed of students from both schools.

Whitwell Middle School and Solomon Schechter Day School students, April 2006

Ben Barker, currently the assistant principal at Whitwell High School, was one of the WMS students who made the trip in 2006. He said, "Our group had been working to learn the songs for the concert, and many of the songs and words were in Hebrew. For us, it was very difficult to do."

Even though the task was difficult, the students rose to Mrs. Hooper's expectations. Ben also noted, "For many, if not all of us, it was the first time we had been on an airplane."

After students arrived in Boston, they were invited to shadow the students from Solomon Schechter Day School. Ben Barker recalled their experiences from that day. "The classes were much smaller, only having eight to ten students. The content was similar to what we were learning. The change in diet for three days was memorable due to the kosher menu. For many of us it was hard to eat unfamiliar food. The group was very interested in sharing their culture with us. We were invited to join a student at his bar mitzvah where there was a lot of music and dancing. It was very different from what we imagined."

The WMS choral students sang with the Schechter students, followed by a speech from Holocaust survivor Sam Natanson. "For all of the words that you hear—this is the action that can make the world a better place," Natanson said about their performance.

Ben Barker explained, "The event was covered by the *Today* show. At the concert we were honored to have the privilege of escorting several Holocaust survivors to the front of the room before singing the songs we had rehearsed."

"When the choirs sing together, the differences fall away," Linda said of her students' work. She was proud of them and overwhelmed by the performance. "You couldn't tell whose voices were whose."

A Trip to Poland

As more people viewed *Paper Clips* and were affected by the poignant documentary, people like Bob Cusick, a financial planner from Cortlandt Manor, New York, wanted to get involved. The film struck Cusick deeply and made him say to his wife Laurie, "I wonder if these kids have ever seen the actual sites?" This curiosity led him to find out they had not.

Cusick embarked on an ambitious fundraising campaign, one that would raise enough money to send ten WMS students and their adult chaperones to Poland. A significant amount of the funding came from the International March of the Living, an organization that funds Holocaust education, with Cusick providing the rest.

According to Cusick, "Mrs. Hooper was admirably and fiercely protective of the students, and it took me some time to get her to accept my honest intentions and authenticity. During the planning of our subsequent trip, over numerous phone calls and emails, I got to know both the master educator and the person, whom I now proudly call a friend."

Although Linda was hesitant about the trip, she could not refuse Cusick's generous gesture. She explained, "After my first trip to Poland and visit to Auschwitz, I was so overwhelmed with grief and with the horror of what was done to the Jews there, I swore that I would never go back. Seeing the tracks just wide enough to carry a body into the crematorium, knowing that the killing continued 24/7 for years, seeing the images of starving victims, thinking of human beings being made to stand in freezing weather for hours, whole rooms filled with human hair, glasses, shoes, and braces that had been taken from the victims of the crematoriums and gas chambers suffocated me. But then, Bob Cusick offered to raise funds to take ten of our students to all the major camps in Poland. How could I deny them the opportunity to see firsthand what intolerance and prejudice could cause?"

Although it was difficult, Linda was determined to see it through. Perhaps by being there herself, she would be able to provide support for the students seeing these things for the first time.

In June of 2011, Linda Hooper, assistant principal Kim Hedrick, and ten students met Bob Cusick at John F. Kennedy Airport in New York. The Whitwell Middle School group in their Tennessee orange shirts was hard to miss, and Bob wore the orange shirt they had given him as well.

While students were waiting for their flight, a Nerf ball being tossed around accidentally set off an alarm at JFK. Bob saw Linda take command of the situation. He saw she could handle this group of restless, rowdy middle schoolers through a foreign country. Bob and the WMS crew set off for Poland. Along with the adult chaperones and students, an interpreter joined them. A film crew from the Johnson group was already on site for another production and filmed portions of the trip for possible use in a subsequent documentary.

When they entered Auschwitz, the students were speechless. It was one thing for them to see photographs, read books, and talk to survivors, but being in the rooms where the atrocities took place was staggering.

The trip to Poland, June 2011. Back row, from left: Kim Hedrick, Linda Hooper, Joe Fab, Kayla Long, Emily Young, Morgan Floyd, Taylor Fike, Emily Malsy, Devin Smith, Bob Cusick, Jessica Privett, and Cassie Yawn. In front: Ricky Chapin and Josh Patton.

One of the students on this trip was Linda's granddaughter, Emily Hooper. Just like her grandmother years before, Emily saw the rooms filled with tangible evidence left behind. "My strongest memory of Auschwitz is seeing the case of human hair that took up an entire room. The case was full of hair that had been shaved from people entering the camp. I think that really made me wrap my mind around what happened at Auschwitz. I also remember seeing mounds of personal items such as shoes and toothbrushes taken from people entering the camp. I realized that each toothbrush belonged to a person who was taken by the Nazis."

A toothbrush implied an opportunity for self-care. A life to live after this interruption was over. However, hope for a future

Whitwell Middle School students and Linda Hooper are filmed at a memorial site in Poland by the Johnson film crew.

ended when most of the Jewish people set foot on the train, even if they didn't know that at the time.

Reflecting on her memories of Auschwitz, Emily said, "The experience definitely brought me closer to my grandmother. It has also helped shape the way I view the world and how I treat other people."

When reflecting on what he wanted others to remember about this venture, Bob Cusick said, "True respect for others, regardless of race, religion, or origin, is best gained through learned experience. While racism and intolerance in every form is reprehensible, experience is the only true teacher to this undeniable point."

Paper Clip Ride
to Remember, 2006

One might wonder what a group of burly motorcyclists would have in common with a small Southern middle school in Tennessee. However, when the school is Whitwell Middle School known for the Children's Holocaust Memorial and the motorcyclists are the Jewish Motorcycle Alliance, the connection is apparent.

According to the Jewish Motorcycle Alliance website, "Each year, riders from each of the member clubs [across the United States], whose numbers have grown from five to thirty-eight, meet in a different city, socialize, ride, interact with members and organizations [of the] local Jewish community, and raise funds in support of a different organization dedicated to Holocaust education and awareness."

In 2006, the cause was Whitwell Middle School's Paper Clips Project. To mark Holocaust Remembrance Day that year, the group met in Chattanooga and rode together to Whitwell. "We are here to honor the students and educators of Whitwell and also to remember the victims of the Holocaust," Stephen Stein, a Ride to Remember organizer said.

On a drizzly day in May, more than two hundred motorcycles roared into the school parking lot, crushing the stereotype of motorcyclists as a hellraising, law-breaking community. Hundreds of students cheered as the riders filed into the gymnasium. "You are educating the world about being tolerant and understanding," Stephen Stein told the students.

Mrs. Hooper and WMS educators welcomed the group and their generous gift of seven electronic Promethean boards to help the educators of Whitwell Middle School continue educating their students with the newest resources of the time.

"They came here to honor our students and to interact with them," Mrs. Hooper said. "The thing that stood out the most was their integrity, commitment to Holocaust education, respect for this project, and their love of adventure."

Jeffrey Kromer and Greg Nisan planned a return visit in 2021, but due to COVID, the visit had to be conducted via Zoom.

An Author Visit in Israel

At the beginning of the Holocaust study group in 1998, Sandra Roberts and David Smith had to gather materials to use. Ms. Roberts found the book *I Have Lived a Thousand Years* about a young girl who survived the Holocaust. She read the book aloud to each study group for twenty years.

Ms. Roberts and the students often wondered what happened to the author, Livia Bitton-Jackson. After a determined internet search, Sandra Roberts finally located her email. She wrote, "Is this you?" and in her excitement, she forgot to include her name. She received a response shortly thereafter that read, "I don't know who 'you' is, but I am Dr. Livia Jackson, author of *I Have Lived a Thousand Years*."

According to Ms. Roberts, Dr. Livia Jackson was one of "the faces and reasons we counted paper clips." She arranged a Skype call in early 2018, and WMS students Skyped with the ninety-year-old Holocaust survivor, then a resident of Israel.

"I see you in person," she said. "All the way from Tennessee."

During the call, students and educators made plans to visit Israel. After gaining approval for the trip and raising enough money, students Grace White, Heidi Worley, and Karsen Hudson were able to travel to Israel in October 2018 with Sandra Roberts, Dr. Josh Holtcamp, and David Smith to meet the elusive and much-admired author. Not only were the students able

From left, Grace Moore, Dr. Leonard Jackson, Dr. Livia Britton-Jackson, Karsen Hudson, and Heidi Worley.

to read the words from her book in the classroom, but they were also able to talk to her face-to-face, ask her questions, give her a hug, and hold her hand. The learning went from a closed classroom experience to the reality of viewing her concentration camp tattoo in person.

In addition to visiting with the author, David Smith and the WMS students engaged a Muslim taxi driver to tour some of Israel's holy sites. The driver taught them about the issues facing Israel and educated them about its history as they traveled around the city. He showed the places where Jesus walked and told stories that solidified the group's Christian faith.

When they entered the Temple Mount, he instructed the males to take off their kippahs, a head covering worn by Jewish men. Non-Muslim religious attire was not permitted, nor were Christian or Jewish prayers. The intense Israeli security around the Western Wall created an awareness for these visitors from Tennessee of the dangers here. This place is considered to be the holiest place for the Jewish people, a place too holy to enter, yet it is controlled by Muslims. In addition to its importance to Jews, it is one of Islam's holiest sites. David Smith felt overwhelmed. Student Heidi Worley was a little scared but "trusted the guards had things under control."

When asked about her takeaway from this experience, Heidi said, "You can't let history get swept under the rug. All these events affect the way the world turns out. Don't let things just stay in a book. Meet the survivors."

Karsen added, "I didn't realize that Israel was such a beautiful place and not just a bombed-out city. It's positive with the nicest people." Karsen also expressed gratitude for those who had donated funds so students could have experiences meeting authors and going to locations relevant to their studies.

For Dr. Joshua Holtcamp, this trip foreshadowed his future role as principal of Whitwell Middle School. "It was on the return trip from Tel Aviv to JFK that I knew I was ready to carry the mantle of WMS principal whenever the opportunity arose. I am proud to represent this school and the project and to change the world, one classroom at a time. Whitwell is my home, and this is my community. We are a small community, but one that can do big things for the betterment of our children."

Learning from Students' Experiences

"It is up to us to keep spreading our message to keep something like the Holocaust from happening again. Time
doesn't repeat itself, but man does."
              – Casey Condra

Casey Condra was one of the students featured prominently
in the documentary *Paper Clips*. The filming began in 2001,
the third year of the Holocaust study group. Once the project
was highlighted by the national news media, the paper clips
flowed in and eventually the project received thirty million
clips. While eleven million are stored in the railcar, the remaining paper clips are given to visitors to the Children's Holocaust
Memorial and to schools who request them.

Casey and his class were filmed in real time as they learned
about the horrors of the Holocaust in front of the documentary
cameras. The rawness of this experience was captured by filmmakers and touched audiences around the world.

The film gave Casey the opportunity to become a public
speaker and "travel the world to speak our message of peace
and tolerance." One of those opportunities was a trip to Germany to visit two concentration camps and speak at fourteen

schools. As an eighth grader from a small rural mining town, Casey traveled the United States speaking in front of large audiences, sometimes consisting of thousands of people.

Even with the serious work of learning about the Holocaust, these students still managed to have fun, sometimes at the expense of the educators. During Halloween one year, Casey and his friends thought "it would be a good idea to throw toilet paper on Linda Hooper's trees at her house. The next morning my mother heard about all the toilet paper on the trees and made me go over there to help clean up the mess she didn't know I created. I always believed Mrs. Hooper knew it was us because of the big grin on her face as we were cleaning it all up."

After Casey graduated from Whitwell High School, he received funds from the Hooper scholarship. He used it to attend the University of Tennessee at Chattanooga, where he graduated with a double major in mathematics and secondary education-mathematics. Currently, he works as operations manager for Advanced Power & Lighting, Inc., in Chattanooga.

More than two decades have passed since he participated in the study group, and Casey still feels the impact from it. "The one thing about the project I love is that it's still evolving."

Although Casey doesn't do railcar tours or travel to speak like he did in the beginning, he is still contacted by people who are viewing the film for the first time. People reach out to him on social media to see how the project is going today.

Casey explained, "The absolute best thing about the project is that it didn't stop after the initial goals were met. Every year there is another group that gets to come in and learn about tolerance and diversity, which keeps that message alive. That's the ultimate goal in my mind, to keep speaking the message from class to class, from generation to generation. It is up to us to keep spreading our message to keep something like the

Holocaust from happening again. Time doesn't repeat itself, but man does."

"*No matter what is happening in the world around you, always be empathetic.***"**
           – Drew Shadrick

As a fourteen-year-old eighth grader at Whitwell Middle School in 2001, Drew Shadrick studied the Holocaust with Sandra Roberts and David Smith. With the attention from the national media focused on the work of the project, Drew honed his social skills with visits from White House correspondents and documentary film crews.

Drew said, "We were interviewed by the *Washington Post* and the *Boston Globe* within days of each other. A normal day in the life of our eighth-grade class was being followed around by cameras or reporters. It was coming to school earlier than we had to and opening letters from all over Europe. It was life changing."

When Linda called him to her office after Christmas break to ask him to attend a conference, he was ready to listen.

"Mrs. Hooper told me of the possibility of going to Austria for a conference, but I would have to go alone, and would I be okay with it. Of course I would, but the question in my mind was, would Mom and Dad allow it? Luckily for me, it was pre-9/11, and they saw it as an amazing opportunity."

Drew spent the next few months preparing for the trip. This preparation allowed Drew to see a different side of his educators. He knew David Smith as a coach and Sandra Roberts as a teacher, friend, and confidante. "[Sandra] was the one we'd be able to just go and talk to about anything."

Drew's experience with Principal Hooper before this trip planning was limited. "Linda—or Mrs. Hooper as I will always call her—was all business, all the time. She could silence an entire gym of preteen kids by clearing her throat, raising her hand, and giving a look. But working in the office before my trip, I got to see a different side of her. During that time, we were getting crates of letters and paper clips every day. I would see her reading the letters and tearing up at some of the stories. I didn't tell the other students because they'd have never believed me—ha ha!"

Drew's trip turned out to be an unexpected adventure for everyone. Drew explains, "Looking back on the trip after it was over, it was a mess. I was traveling with my luggage and also a comically large box full of trinkets (for lack of a better term) from Tennessee to pass out at the conference. I was supposed to have an escort to take me from my flight into Frankfurt to my connecting flight to Vienna. When I got off the plane, there was no one there. Somehow, I fumbled around through the airport and found my flight.

"When I arrived in Vienna, I was to have a family that I would stay with the first night and the last night of the trip. What I didn't know was that in Austria outsiders are not allowed to be at baggage claim, and the windows to the outside world were completely blacked out. So, after I picked up my bag and box, I looked for almost two hours for the family, crying for about an hour of that. I tried calling home, but since this was before cellphones were the norm, I had to try to use a pay phone. I couldn't get it to work. After about two hours, I decided that I was going through the door and would figure it out once I got outside. The family was just on the other side of the door and had been just as panicked as I was!"

After this hiccup, Drew's trip continued as planned. He was the youngest person at the conference by at least eight years. Attendees were given a tour of the Mauthausen Concentration Camp.

During the day, attendees worked on a children's memorial at the Mauthausen Concentration Camp. The goal of the conference was for the attendees to make something to leave with the main exhibit, an abstract wooden statue of a child. Drew chose to make a paper clip for his contribution.

They met their goal to finish the memorial by the Liberation Day Ceremony in May 2001. "The day before the celebration we took an extended tour of the concentration camp, the rock quarry, and the museum. ... The rock quarry was terrible. The prisoners would have to mine limestone and carry boulders up a set of stairs they dubbed the Stairway of Death. I urge readers to Google the camp and read about it."

The evenings were spent discussing tolerance, the topic of the conference. Drew explains, "The nightly talks were very spirited. There were people from Ireland, Germany, the Czech Republic, England, Austria, and me from the US. All different ages and backgrounds. There were musicians, university students, social workers, and even a chef. On the night I presented the [WMS] Holocaust project, I passed out the trinkets that I brought—a Moon Pie, small Coca-Cola, an airplane bottle of Jack Daniels, a Lodge cast iron ashtray, Goo Goo Clusters, and an American flag. The group laughed at the flag and said they'd expect nothing less from an American.

"The conference was a success, and at the end of it, a few of the members told me that they were glad to finally meet an American and that I'd changed their views of us a little. Apparently, I wasn't as overconfident or full of myself as they expected."

Today, after a couple of years as a neonatal intensive care unit nurse and a career change, Drew is working his dream job as a maintenance engineering manager at the Magic Kingdom in Walt Disney World. His journey to get to that goal was influenced by his experiences at WMS. When asked how the Holocaust project changed him, he replied, "Empathy. No matter what is happening in the world around you, always be empathetic."

When Drew listened to a group of Holocaust survivors at WMS, one of the men spoke about counting the lice in the bed he slept in for entertainment. He explains, "I believe this lesson helped me to be a better NICU nurse and now helps me when helping guests at the Magic Kingdom. You never know what else is happening in a person's life, and a smile and a simple gesture can make all the difference."

"*Our students were struggling with meeting different cultures and people outside of our little valley. After the project, students knew how to find common ground, how to speak with people from other places, and found lots of success in jobs helping the public.*"

– Taylor McDaniel Kilgore

Taylor Kilgore was in the fifth grade when the Children's Holocaust Memorial became a reality, only a few weeks after September 11. "As a ten-year-old, I watched as news outlets replayed the Twin Towers collapsing, carrying the shock of the terrorist attacks across an astonished world. In the days and weeks after September 11, the world, and my childhood as I knew it, shifted. However, in my small corner of Tennessee, not all was dark.

"Only a month later, I watched, mesmerized, as a railcar slowly descended onto tracks in front of my school. Cheers erupted from the massive crowd. Amid tragedy and terror, this railcar, once used to transport prisoners to concentration and death camps during World War II, had completed its final journey."

Taylor's love of history was ignited that day. "When that time came [to join the Holocaust study group in eighth grade], I gave tours of the car, traveled across the Southeast to speak about my experiences, sang at the lighting of the National Christmas Tree in 2004 with my classmates, and met people from around the world. I even came back as a senior during my service-learning class to help file letters and give tours. This project, quite literally, made me who I am today."

With Taylor's passion for history as the foundation, she graduated from Cumberland University with a degree in history and a license to teach. She returned to Whitwell Middle School to teach eighth grade U.S. History and to co-teach the Paper Clips Project. Taylor reflected on the journey from Holocaust study group member to educator. "There are so many things you learn as a part of the Holocaust study group that it is hard to list. And the intriguing part about it is that, as a student, you don't realize it. I didn't realize the lessons until I was in college, and David [Smith] came to speak to my class. My small town had broadened my horizons more than some of my city-raised friends—and I didn't know until I was much older."

With her degree completed, Taylor "realized it was my turn to step in my teacher's shoes." Having participated in the project as a student herself, Taylor understands the deep emotions students encounter for the first time. Listening to survivor stories with her students, she watches them grapple with the cruelty of humans, wiping away tears and encouraging them as they grow in self-confidence as they learn to stand up for their beliefs.

With testing mandates gaining prominence in US schools, Taylor addressed the issue: "A test will never measure what my students are learning from this project. Our students were struggling with meeting different cultures and people outside of our little valley. After the project, students knew how to find common ground, how to speak with people from other places, and found lots of success in jobs helping the public. We have educators, doctors and nurses, therapists, and many other social jobs." Taylor also points out that "goals for our students don't always revolve around a test score. Becoming a better human, teaching empathy, growth in self-confidence, and learning from people around the world will never be measured by a test."

With the retirement of Linda Hooper and Sandra Roberts, Taylor McDaniel Kilgore agreed to lead the Holocaust study group. Her plans for the future include making the letters and memorabilia available digitally. "Not everyone can travel to Whitwell to visit the memorial. If the materials are online, everyone can view them," Taylor explained.

"People in a bubble of like-minded individuals will never grow mentally or personally, but I was able to escape that scenario through the project."*

– Dalton Slatton

Dalton was raised on Whitwell Mountain, a rural Appalachian community even smaller than the town of Whitwell. Civic engagement was not a priority for his family. Other than a grandmother who voted occasionally, Dalton's family was not registered to vote until he took them in 2018.

When asked about what inspired him, he said, "I realized how important every vote is. No matter who or what you cast your vote for, it is everyone's civic duty to be a part of the system that makes the rules that affect us. I also didn't feel like I could encourage other people to vote with my own family not registered."

From the time he visited the railcar in elementary school, Dalton knew he wanted to be a part of the project. He explained, "As an eighth grader, I was in charge of giving tours of the railcar when groups came. I spent a lot of time learning the story of the railcar from its time as a vehicle for death and despair until its revitalization as a memorial in honor of those it once transported to concentration camps. I treated the railcar as the solemn memorial it is. There wasn't and still isn't a time I don't enter without giving reverence to the lives that it represents as a final resting place."

As part of the tour, visitors to the Children's Holocaust Memorial railcar outside the school building are given access to the Holocaust Artifacts Library, which was created to store the memorabilia sent from around the world to memorialize the victims. It is stuffed full and gets fuller. One artifact that touched Dalton was an authentic World War II prisoner's jacket. "It's battered, worn, torn, and we know that real people wore this in a camp. It brings a sense of somberness to the room."

While a student at Whitwell High School, Dalton had the opportunity to travel to Washington, DC, with Linda to participate in One Million Bones, a social awareness project that combines education, hands-on art-making, and public installations to bring awareness to on-going genocide.

"The National Mall looked like a cemetery with bones made of cloth, paper, and flour," Dalton explained. Whitwell contributed ten thousand of those bones baked in churches and homes throughout the town by a community willing to help.

The cultural exposure didn't end with participation in the project. When other students chose to go to McDonald's for lunch, Dalton chose to stay with Mrs. Hooper and purchase food from a nearby Vietnamese food truck. This was Dalton's first food truck and East Asian food experience. Dalton remembered, "The beet and carrot slaw [was] delicious on my sandwich."

Dalton also traveled to Philadelphia numerous times representing Whitwell Middle School. "Two families that I particularly became close to were the Einhorns and the Kestenbaums. Both families live in the Philadelphia area. I spent a great amount of time in the Philadelphia area during my high school career on behalf of the project."

When visiting with the Einhorns (Norman, Deb, Ethan, Alli, and dog Sammy), Dalton said, "I was treated as part of the family. During those times, if I wasn't speaking to a group, we made time for a movie, nice dinner, or even a snowball fight once when it snowed. Our travels took us to Ocean City, New Jersey, to enjoy the boardwalk and New York City to watch a musical on Broadway."

The Kestenbaum family (Joseph, Sharon, and their five children David, Matthew, Eli, Sarah, and Jacob) welcomed Dalton into their home as well. "The joke became I was the sixth child because I fit so perfectly between David and Matthew in age."

During Dalton's downtime, the Kestenbaums introduced him to hockey, attempting to teach him to ice skate and taking him to a Philadelphia Flyers hockey game.

Dalton's relationship with these families didn't end once his tenure as a Paper Clips ambassador ended. "Both of these families hold a special place in my heart and have never ceased being there for me to celebrate my accomplishments or to give a word of encouragement."

With help from the Hooper Scholarship, Dalton graduated debt-free from Middle Tennessee State University and received his law degree at the oldest law school in the country, William & Mary Law School. He is currently serving in the US Judge Advocate General's (JAG) Corps.

Dalton reflects on the impact of the project on his life: "The project challenged me as a teenager to look beyond the city limits of Whitwell and experience the world. At the impressionable ages I spent traveling with the project, I met people and had experiences that I would never have had access to without being in the project."

Instead of being scared or intimidated by the differences in people, Dalton was curious. "People in a bubble of like-minded individuals will never grow mentally or personally, but I was able to escape that scenario through the project." Dalton's eyes were opened to possibilities outside the small town of Whitwell. "The project and experiences made me check my biases when living in a small Southern town."

As a Children's Holocaust Memorial volunteer alumni, Dalton's education went beyond the four walls of the classroom to encompass a passion for those threatened with genocide, a desire to have his family participate in the election process, and a dedication to serve others with his law degree.

"Seeing what life is like from a different perspective is a challenging lesson on learn."

– Morgan Floyd

Morgan Floyd was born into a family with roots entrenched in the mountains of Whitwell. Morgan was raised with the echoes of eighteen-wheelers laden down with coal rumbling down the mountain. Even though the mines had closed years before he was born, community conversation still embraced the mines like a beloved family member who had passed away. Whispers of good-paying jobs, "when the mines were open," dotted conversations, and even the explosion of Tennessee Consolidated Coal Mine # 21 that killed thirteen miners added to the mystique for those who worked there and survived.

With this history as his foundation, Morgan Floyd is part of a new generation of youth rising up from the antiquated past, a generation willing to try new things and embrace new ideas out of curiosity and necessity.

When Morgan was given the opportunity to join the Paper Clips Project, he didn't hesitate. Morgan explains, "Seeing what life is like from a different perspective is a challenging lesson to learn. However, this project instills the importance of acceptance at an early age."

Serving as a tour guide for the Children's Holocaust Memorial allowed Morgan the opportunity to meet and talk with a diverse group of people he would have never encountered in the small, rural town of Whitwell, Tennessee.

In addition to the stained-glass windows, Morgan had a hand in creating a paper clips quilt that now hangs in the hallway at WMS.

According to Morgan, "Traveling to Poland was the most impactful part of my time in the project. Watching movies and reading stories is no comparison to seeing the actual reason why the Paper Clips Project exists."

Perspectives from Two Inspiring Women

Curiosity about the Paper Clips Project led two women to Linda Hooper, reaching out for different reasons, yet seeking the same thing: hope. Both were surprised that the WMS principal took time to speak with them. Jennie Zagnoev and Stephanie Zhong were at different stages in their lives when they reached out to Linda for answers.

Jennie Zagnoev was a sixteen-year-old sophomore in high school, Jewish, and born and raised in Nashville. In the spring of 2000, she had just returned from the March of the Living, whose goals include "remembering the six million Jews who perished in the Shoah."

Jennie's mother gave her an article from *Tennessean* magazine about Whitwell Middle School and their intention to collect 6,000,000 paper clips, one for each of the Jews killed during the Holocaust. Jennie felt a kinship with those students "who were so interested in learning about what is part of my culture."

Jennie's mother encouraged her to call Linda Hooper. Jennie explained, "So, I did. It really was that simple. I called, asked to speak with her, and within seconds, she came right to the phone. I told her that I had read the article and about my recent trip. In her sweet Southern accent, she invited me to come speak with the current Holocaust class about my experience."

A couple of weeks later, Jennie Zagnoev was sharing her March of the Living experience with WMS students in the Holocaust study group. After the presentation, Linda shared her plan to acquire a railcar used to transport people to concentration camps. It would be used to house the 6,000,000 paper clips.

"This was truly the moment I got involved, I think. I asked her how much the railcar would cost to prepare the car to display the clips, and she told me. I quickly told her that I would help get the money. From that instant, I began to reach out to family and friends. I wanted to be part of the project. I wanted to help them fulfill their dreams and meet their goal. I raised over $15,000 for the school over the next several months. At the dedication of the railcar in Whitwell, TN, I saw it. Their vision came to life. Several years of hard work, learning, and teaching had come full circle. We did it together."

While Jennie Zagnoev was directly involved with assisting in the project before the *Paper Clips* film, Stephanie Zhong began sharing the message years later during an unsettled political climate. After the 2012 presidential election, Stephanie wrote, "I was losing hope for our country when I suddenly remembered the *Paper Clips* film and watched it again on Amazon.

"At the time I wanted to develop a story about everyday people bridging differences and decided to reach out to Linda for an interview to find out what happened to the kids and the project." Stephanie and Linda spoke on the phone for ninety minutes, "like two kindred spirits having tea in her kitchen."

As an Asian-American, Stephanie explained, "I have always struggled to feel like I belong even though I was born and raised here." Her preconceived notion of young, white Southern kids was shattered after meeting and speaking with students involved with the project. "I was surprised to see a group of eighth graders from rural Tennessee go to such lengths to learn about a group of people totally different from them." Their open-mindedness "moved me to believe that despite painful histories and trauma, we might just be able to build bridges to each other."

Students from Whitwell Middle School are not only learning about other cultures, but they are educating the world about negative Appalachian stereotypes as well. In response, Stephanie created a podcast called *One Small Thing,* and is now a story brand coach offering help for those who need communication guidance.

3

The Legacy
of Paper Clips

Alan 'Ace' Greenberg
Creates a Scholarship

When Alan "Ace" Greenberg's office called Whitwell Middle School in June of 2005 about making a $500,000 donation, Linda thought they were being scammed. Secretaries were instructed to make excuses because she wouldn't take the calls. Just like with the first phone calls from Ari Pinchot about making the documentary, Linda avoided these calls until one day she was at work earlier than staff and answered the school phones. She spoke with Mr. Greenberg's executive secretary and agreed to talk to him. Later, she was glad she did.

When Mr. Greenberg told Mrs. Hooper that he wanted to donate a half-million dollars for scholarships, she accepted the offer but still didn't quite believe it. The next day when the students and staff returned to school, she told the secretary that "some guy had called and said he was sending a check for a half-million dollars." She never expected to see the check, so when it was delivered the next day by FedEx, she told the bookkeeper to rush it to the bank. If the check didn't bounce, she would call Mr. Greenberg, write him a thank you note, and invite him to visit Whitwell Middle School.

A half-million-dollar donation was just beyond anything she had ever encountered. She took the time to look Mr. Greenberg up on the internet, discovering that he was the head of Bear Stearns, a successful investment company located in New York City. That Ace Greenberg knew about the Paper Clips Project a thousand miles away in Whitwell, Tennessee, was incredible. The fact he was going to provide a half-million dollars for scholarships to students at the local high school left her speechless. She was especially humbled that he wanted the recipients to be called Hooper Scholars.

What Linda didn't know was that Mr. Greenberg had just viewed the documentary and was stirred by the work done by the students of Whitwell Middle School and impressed by her leadership. "What Mrs. Hooper did is amazing," Greenberg said. "This is really moving."

When Linda met Mr. Greenberg later at his office in New York City, she corrected him on his compliments, telling him that she was simply a "cat herder," that the real work had been done by the students, the staff, and the community with the blessing of a higher power.

Ace was gracious and totally attentive to the information she had to offer. Linda was overwhelmed by the fact that a person of his stature would take the time not only to listen to her but to just chat as one human to another with her and her son Scott, who had accompanied her to New York. Ace did not rush the visit. He was simply engaged human to human. This entire interaction only confirmed Linda's belief that a far higher power has always been in charge of this project.

A few months later Mr. Greenberg came for a visit to Whitwell Middle School. During the visit, this head of Bear Stearns and successful global banker performed a magic show for the students. The students were mesmerized and intrigued by the fact that this famous person was doing a magic act at their school. According to Linda, "He was a lovely, gracious human who made me examine my own stereotypes about people. Ace totally crushed my stereotype of an investment titan. Years later I learned that he encouraged all his employees to contribute a part of their salary to projects dedicated to alleviating the world's problems."

From 2002 until 2024, the seed money of $500,000 to the Hooper Scholarship fund had aided one hundred six students. To qualify for the scholarship, the student had to attend Whitwell High School and complete 144 public service hours. Once enrolled in college, students have to maintain a 2.5 GPA and possess good attendance records. The average amount of the scholarship awarded has been $1,000 per year per student.

Har Zion School and Whitwell Middle School

When Norman Einhorn, principal of Har Zion School for Jewish Studies in Philadelphia, heard about the Paper Clips Project from a congregant in 2011, he was intrigued. "I watched the film with two students I was tutoring, and it blew me away—the rest is history.... I couldn't let it go."

Soon after, conversations began between project leader Sandra Roberts and Mr. Einhorn. She was invited to Philadelphia to speak to his students about the film and the work still taking place at Whitwell Middle School. Mr. Einhorn recounted, "We were so overcome with emotion and instant love when Sandy came to speak, and we screened the film as a community."

That contact led to visit after visit between WMS and Har Zion students. Einhorn explained, "It has been a gift and a blessing to welcome teachers and students into my home and into our community ... and I feel equally as blessed that I have been welcomed with open arms in Whitwell as well. My Whitwell family truly is part of my extended family."

Part of this time was spent learning about the culture of the other community. WMS students like Kayla Long, "helped plan and set up for groups such as those from Har Zion High School and Synagogue." As a result, lasting friendships were formed.

One of these visits Har Zion made to Whitwell included a delivery of 669 boxes of cereal and a $2,100 check for the Marion County Food Bank.

This unlikely friendship not only benefited the students from both schools but continues to spread awareness about the importance of the project while serving the local food bank as well.

"This project is bigger than any one person. It makes me sad to say this," Einhorn points out, "but sometimes I think that society still hasn't learned the lessons of the Holocaust and the long-standing relationship between our two communities serves as a beacon of light and hope during tough times."

WMS Holocaust Artifacts Library

People who learned about the project were moved to go beyond emails and letters. They saw that the Children's Holocaust Memorial could be trusted as a repository for family artifacts and memorabilia. Just as paper clips had flowed in, donations of treasured keepsakes flowed in.

When visitors enter Whitwell Middle School, stained-glass windows are the first thing to catch their eye. With a grant from the Tennessee Arts Commission the windows were painstakingly crafted by WMS students who were trained in the art of stained glass by local artists Sara Moore and Jackie Lofty.

As a result of his involvement in the Paper Clips Project, student Morgan Floyd also had the opportunity to create stained glass windows for the foyer outside the Holocaust Artifacts Library at Whitwell Middle School. The artifacts room is attached to the school library directly across from the main office and houses the largest library of Holocaust literature in the Southeast. Morgan worked on windows that depicted the paper clips journey. It gave him a chance to "be a part of something that was art related and showcased such an amazing project."

Morgan explained, "The days our group would meet were my favorite days of the week! We would attend school as usual,

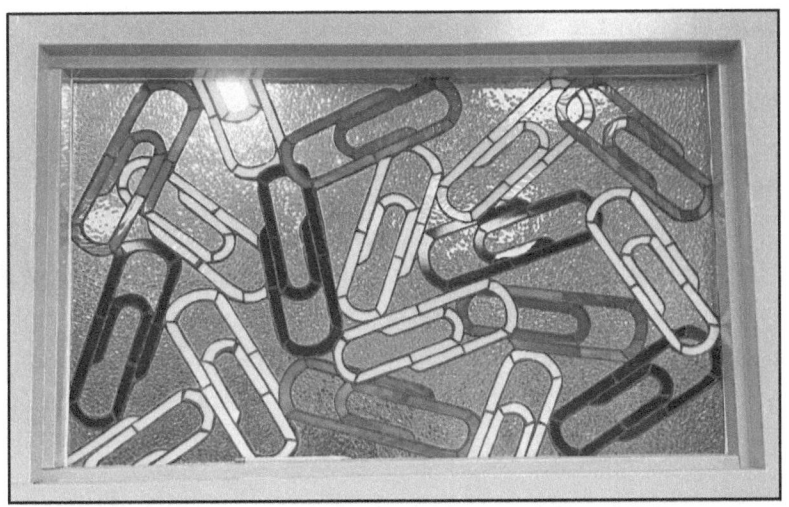

A stained glass window of paper clips in the foyer outside the Holocaust Artifacts Library.

Stained glass windows outside the artifacts library.

Star of David stained glass window in the foyer outside the artifacts library.

then head to the office to work on our projects. We general-ly had two windows that we would work on at a time. Emily Hooper [Malsy]and I were the two that stuck with the project from start to finish, however, we had some other classmates to help us along the way as well."

To the right of the WMS foyer, above the entry door of the Holocaust Artifacts Library are more stained-glass windows with images of paper clips, butterflies, and the railcar, all com-memorating the work done by the school. Jackie Lofty also ren-ovated the butterfly stepping stones at the railcar that had been damaged by the weather.

After careful consideration of the vast assortment of artifacts, the students determined that the items portrayed in stained glass were especially significant. They chose these items because "they encompass the history, the heartbreak, and the diversity of the suffering the Jewish people experienced during the Ho-locaust."

The room houses treasures shared by people all over the world, notebooks containing over thirty thousand letters and emails, and memorabilia from the making of the *Paper Clips* documentary.

The letters and emails preserved in the Holocaust Artifacts Library came from all seven continents and fill over 150 note-books. The German letters were translated by Susan Gruber and her mother, Gisela Redick. Each one of them was answered by students—except for the letters from Holocaust deniers.

The treasures came from survivors and their families, from US soldiers who liberated camps at the end of World War II, and from people who had collected items and needed a safe place to store and display them.

Propaganda poster on display in the Holocaust Artifacts Library: First Lieutenant Vernon R. Wolcott helped liberate the Landsberg concentration camp, a satellite camp of Dachau, in April 1945. As one of the first GIs to enter the camp, Wolcott was an eyewitness to the Nazi atrocities in Landsberg, known for being the location of the jail cell where Adolf Hitler wrote Mein Kampf. *Wolcott took pictures to document these atrocities. He then sent these pictures and the propaganda poster back to his parents with a handwritten note at the bottom explaining what he saw. His account, eyewitness pictures, and camera were donated to the Children's Holocaust Memorial by the family after First Lieutenant Wolcott passed away.*

A typical jacket worn by concentration camp inmates. The red triangle represents the "crime" for which the inmate was held. The white strip has two handwritten numbers on it. This indicated the jacket was worn by two different people. The last person was a political prisoner, as indicated by the color of the triangle. The items were all donated by Dr. Lon Nuell.

The tambourine and footprints made with cut Torah pages are symbols of Nazi attempts to destroy a culture as well as its people. By forcing Jewish prisoners to cut up sacred texts of the Torah to create musical instruments or to stand on the texts and cut footprints out was meant to damage more than just the human being standing there.

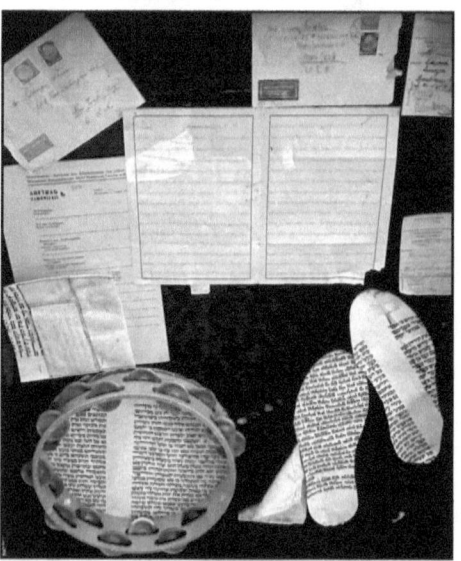

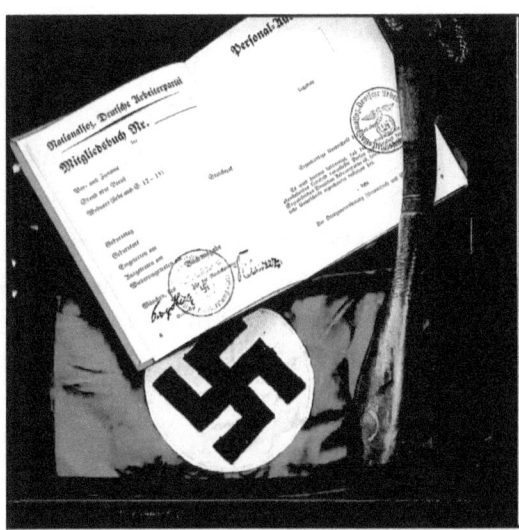

*A Nazi armband,
blackjack,
and notebook
"liberated" by
James Garner Sr.
The blackjack was
from Dachau.*

A framed yellow star of David was donated to Whitwell Middle School by the person who was forced to wear it. This star, encased in a frame on the library wall, is small but it is a massive symbol of atrocities that took place in the Holocaust. The star was used to deny jobs to Jews, isolating them from schools and their communities.

The writing enclosed with the star stated, "On September 1, 1941, the Nazi Reich Minister of the Interior ordered that as of September 19, 1941, Jews over six years of age must wear the Star of David when appearing in public. The Star of David must be a black six-pointed star on yellow material, as big as the palm

of the hand and with the inscription 'Jude' in black. The star had to be worn firmly sewn above the heart and visibly worn on the left breast of clothing." Later, Jews were required to post the Star of David on their doors.

One of the most touching items in the collection is a pink mesh lunch box containing 15,000 tiny paper butterflies, to honor the memory of the children who lost their lives at Terezin. While these children were in this horrible situation, a teacher named Friedl Dicker-Brandeis began to scavenge any items from beets to lumps of coal that the children could use to create artwork as an outlet for their suffering. She saved their work and it survived. After the war, Czech art historian Hana Volavková compiled the art into the book *I Never Saw Another Butterfly*. It takes its title from a poem written by one of the young boys there. The box was given to the Children's Holocaust Memorial by a group of fifth graders from Long Island, NY.

One of the very special artifacts is a Torah brought to CHM by Hymie and Hazel Amoils. This Torah began its journey in Poswohl, Lithuania. Later it traveled with Jewish immigrants to Johannesburg, South Africa, where it rested until the mid-1990s. At that time, the Amoils brought it to Toronto, Canada. Unfortunately, it was not suitable for use in a synagogue.

When the Amoils learned about the Children's Holocaust Memorial, they contacted Linda Hooper and asked if the group would like to have it on display. The response was a resounding *yes*, and the Torah came to its final home in October 2007.

The community was thrilled to receive this gift, which would become a wonderful teaching tool to show the students how its text was a portion of the Christian Bible. Whitwell Middle School did not have an appropriate place for the Torah until the Hebrew Day School in Chattanooga donated an ark that had been refurbished by Chattanooga's Jewish community. While some arks are elaborate, this donated ark was a simple wooden one.

As visitors explore the sacred space, they might miss the sculpture in front of the west window. This Tree of Life was given to the library by Martin Small's widow, Doris. Martin Small was a survivor of the Mauthausen Concentration Camp. Eighty-six paper clips hang from the tree, honoring the members of his family who perished in the Holocaust. He finished making it on his fiftieth wedding anniversary and presented it to his wife. It was his wish that the tree be donated to the Children's Holocaust Memorial. Martin died of pancreatic cancer November 29, 2008.

A Hebrew prayer and song used in Martin's synagogue each week are inscribed on the base of the sculpture. From Proverbs 3:18: "It is a Tree of Life for those who cling to it, and all who uphold it are blessed."

Although this family lost loved ones, their legacy lives on every time a visitor stops in front of the tree and touches one of the eighty-six paper clips.

The Holocaust Artifacts Library houses the largest collection of Holocaust-related literature in the Southeast. Many of the books were donated by Dr. Benjamin Nachman, a dentist in Omaha, Nebraska, before his death in 2010.

One new addition to the artifacts room is the book *And Every Single One Was Someone*, written by Phil Chernofsky. The book contains the word "Jew" written in tiny type six million times. In a *New York Times* interview, the author explained, "When you look at this at a distance, you can't tell whether it's upside down or right-side up, you can't tell what's here; it looks like a pattern. That's how the Nazis viewed their victims: 'These are not individuals; these are not people; these are just a mass we have to exterminate.'"

This book is cherished by student volunteers at WMS. One student tour guide, Grace White, was deeply affected by the book. As she has led tours and educates visitors, she would open the book, point to a page, and speak from the heart, "This book has the word Jew in it six million times. Each word was a person. They had a life, a family, a lifestyle. They were still terminated, no matter what."

One Clip at a Time

When Alison Lebovitz visited the railcar in 2002 with her young son, the Children's Holocaust Memorial instilled a source of deep pride. She was amazed "that a group of students could have such a huge impact on the world." The fact that the students at Whitwell Middle School not only took the time to study the Holocaust but also then asked important questions and found answers awed this Jewish woman from Chattanooga.

Alison felt like she belonged in this small country town. Her first meeting with Linda Hooper was *"B'sheret,"* Linda's favorite Yiddish word meaning "destiny."

Even after Alison Lebovitz watched the documentary *Paper Clips*, she knew the project didn't end there. Linda Hooper agreed. While collecting six million paper clips to honor the Jewish lives lost in the Holocaust was an outstanding achievement, they both knew that education must continue, not just with the educators and students at Whitwell Middle School. They believed training should be offered to any educator who wanted to teach the Holocaust in his or her classroom. It would take some time, conversation, and planning before this common objective would come to fruition.

With that goal in mind, Michael Lebovitz, Alison's brother-in-law, organized a brainstorming session in the summer of 2007 and invited Alison, Linda Hooper, Sandra Roberts, and

Matthew Hiltzik to discuss how to get the *Paper Clips* documentary into more schools.

According to Alison, "There had been several efforts going on towards this end, but none of them coordinated or sanctioned by the school. We left that session in agreement. There needed to be a nonprofit entity formed that would solely concentrate on this mission. We even named it One Clip at a Time to honor the mantra of the project itself."

A few months later in November 2007, Alison explained, "Linda was speaking at a women's luncheon at the General Assembly, a huge Jewish Federation conference, in Nashville, and at the end of her talk she mentioned the potential formation of this new nonprofit. I was stationed at the event to collect postcards that the women were given to fill out if they had any interest in supporting such an organization. The response was overwhelmingly positive, and I felt energized by the surge and enthusiasm the room generated."

Alison stepped into the role of president for the nonprofit and proceeded to raise money through a Community Foundation grant and a donation from the Lebovitz Family Trust that covered the cost of the start-up and teacher training.

Alison sought out educators to get their input as well. After all, they would be teaching this curriculum in their classrooms. The documentary runs for an hour and twenty minutes. At that length, it did not fit into the standard class length of sixty or ninety minutes. The bones of the curriculum were there, but it needed to be repackaged for the classroom.

Alison explained, "After that initial meeting I asked each of the experts to go home, watch the documentary again, and see if the film had any natural breaks. I thought maybe there was a way for us to show a single portion at a time. A week later we gathered, and all agreed there were in fact four natural breaks in the documentary, which would allow us to divide the film into five easy-to-watch parts."

With the five parts chosen, lesson plans were created to align with each one. The lesson plans incorporated service learning and encouraged students as leaders in their communities and classrooms.

A two-day professional development institute was originally developed by Joyce Tatum and Alison Lebovitz and began in the summer of 2008. Currently, the professional development training with the One Clip at a Time program is led by Alison Lebovitz and Greg Knowles. According to Lebovitz, there needed to be a nonprofit entity formed that would solely concentrate on the mission of getting *Paper Clips* into more schools.

Teachers can attend a two-day summer institute that includes one day in Chattanooga and one day on site at the memorial or attend the virtual institute online. There are five lessons included in the training. Above all, this program teaches that education is a call to action.

The first lesson introduces the concept that individuals can make a difference. It also tries to provide an understanding of the consequences of intolerance and prejudice.

The second lesson explores how one person's actions impact other people and the world.

The third lesson looks at the consequences of personal choice.

The fourth lesson develops an understanding of the power of symbols and how symbols may strengthen stereotypes.

The fifth lesson helps students recognize their personal responsibility in creating the world they want to live in.

Matthew Hiltzik, filmmaker and distributor of *Paper Clips*, praised Leibovitz for helping sustain the project. "We were all so fortunate that Alison Leibovitz and her family, who are leaders in the relatively nearby Chattanooga community, saw the same thing we all did in the project, and she dedicated so many resources—time, creativity, and finances—to establish the One Clip at a Time nonprofit. Alison and her colleagues have worked so hard to imagine and actualize a program that uses this film and this project to inspire other educators from around the country to dream with their own students and communities to realize other programs teaching about truth and tolerance, in whatever form they might find."

With the One Clip training and curriculum now available internationally, students all over the world are benefiting from the experiences of the students at Whitwell Middle School. The nonprofit's website (oneclipatatime.org) explains the philosophy behind the nonprofit. "We believe education is a call to action and that every student has the potential to make a difference. Our goal is to help foster an understanding and appreciation of diverse interests, cultures, and backgrounds in students. But more than just giving them the tools they need to combat prejudice, hatred, and discrimination, we are also empowering them to be good stewards and to make positive changes in their own communities. We are creating young philanthropists and future leaders who will convey these lessons to their children and future generations."

When Alison and Linda look back on what has been accomplished with One Clip, they both agree on one thing: God oversees this project. *B'sheret.*

Linda Hooper's New Dream

THE WHITWELL EDUCATION AND HERITAGE CENTER

The documentary *Paper Clips* concluded with the arrival of the authentic German railcar procured by Peter and Dagmar Schroeder at the old Whitwell Middle School. Students cheered and welcomed the railcar that would house the millions of paper clips collected by students over the course of creating the Children's Holocaust Memorial.

When the new Whitwell Middle School was built in 2008, the memorial was moved, so it once again graced the front of the school.

Now, Linda's vision is to establish an education and heritage center that can house the artifacts in a suitable space. The building she imagines will also house the local public library, the local coal miners' museum, the veterans museum, the Holocaust Artifacts Library, and the senior citizens center. This move would fulfill several goals she has in mind, not just for students, but for the whole town of Whitwell too.

Whitwell is a small town with limited financial resources. When Highway 28 was built, the downtown slowly disappeared. Linda explained, "Unlike other nearby towns, Whitwell has no focal point where its citizens can gather for educational and social purposes. Therefore, it is proposed that we create the Whitwell Education and Heritage Center to overcome this issue."

While having the Children's Holocaust Memorial and Artifacts Library at the school is educational, giving students an opportunity to lead tours, it is limiting at the same time. The memorial attracts visitors. A memorial attached to a public school in the process of educating children cannot easily accommodate everyone who wants to come. Spontaneous visits to the school are disruptive and a security risk. Visitors must and should be vetted before they are allowed on school property. Taking these precautions are necessary but also limiting to guests who want to view and appreciate the work done by these students.

The memorial's authentic German railcar is fragile and heavy foot traffic could damage it. The artifacts room is attached to the school library directly across from the main office. Even though the artifacts room houses the largest library of Holocaust literature in the Southeast, the public may only visit it when scheduled through the school at a safe and convenient time.

Another cause for concern is that most small museums don't survive. When the original founders of these institutions can no longer work, fundraise, or manage activities, the museum usually dies. One solution is to encourage more stakeholders to become involved so the passion for the project lives on.

Sustaining the Children's Holocaust Museum is a priority to Linda Hooper, so she has brainstormed with other community

leaders about the possibilities. Not only did they look at the Children's Holocaust Museum, but they also factored in other community needs and resources that could be linked together. Whitwell has many resources to offer. It is a community of loving, caring, generous people who have demonstrated over and over their willingness to provide volunteer labor for worthwhile projects.

Resources include a small coal-mining museum currently located at the old Whitwell Library. Coal mining was once a bustling industry that employed many men in Whitwell and the surrounding area. The decline of coal sales and the deadly explosion at Tennessee Consolidated Coal's Mine No. 21 led to the closure of area mines.

Although local government funds are not available for the establishment of this visible town center, it is Linda's belief and vision "that where there's a will, there's a way." With verbal support from individuals and groups, she is confident that the funding will be secured.

Linda explained, "The establishment of this center would create an area where people could celebrate their heritage and enjoy the educational and social benefits provided by the coal miners' museum, artifacts room, veterans' museum, local library, and senior citizens center. The Whitwell Library and senior citizens center being near each other would provide easy access for community volunteers. Veterans would have a permanent meeting place and space to display their honors and artifacts. The proximity of the Children's Holocaust Memorial to the library and senior citizens center would provide opportunities for community volunteers to give tours at hours when students are not available. This location would also increase security and visibility of this valuable resource. It would demonstrate how accepting our community is and how we work together with limited resources to educate our children and the world about the evils of prejudice. The citizens of Whitwell have used their power to change the world. With the power of the citizens and interested parties, we can allow Whitwell to become all it was meant to be."

> For more information about the Whitwell Education and Heritage Center, visit the following website: **www.whitwellcenter.org**.

APPENDIX

Poems, Songs, Quotes, Reflections

The Holocaust study group resulted in the Paper Clips Project, which generated the Children's Holocaust Memorial. These endeavors have given students a voice in their learning. It has encouraged them to examine their stereotypes about other cultures and demonstrated to them the incredible power that one person possesses to change the world, one act at a time. But most importantly, being a part of this project has shown them the consequences of choices as is so eloquently voiced in this poem.

The Gift of Choice

I came into this world without being asked
And when the time for dying comes
I shall not be consulted
But between the boundaries of birth and death
Lies the Dominion of Choice
To be a doer or a dreamer
To be a lifter or a leaner
To speak out or remain silent
To extend a hand in friendship
Or to look the other way
To feel the suffering of others
Or to be callous and insensitive
These are the choices
It is in the choosing
That my measure as a person
Is Determined.

– Gertrude Hildreth Housman

In This Car

Diesel fumes and cracking wood
Cold steel tracks and nothing good
Mid the tears and burning eyes
Slam the door—hear their cries

Scorching iron of the wheels
They could not speak—
There were no deals
In the shadows they all stood—
Cold steel tracks and nothing good

On to Auschwitz, Treblinka, and hell
So very few were left to tell
Of that time we honor today
But we thank God-
There's more to say

For as we stand—united here
We honor them with every tear
For in this car is light and love
And God's own mercy from up above

We place this monument
On hallowed ground
For all to come and stand around
And touch the place where they once stood
Open the door—there's something good!

– Judge Bob Moon
October 4, 2001

All living things are connected by a bond
Both resilient and fragile
Why man refuses to honor that bond is a question that looms
    larger.

–Bo Niles

I am nothing,
Yet I am everything,
I am the sorrow
I am the pain,
I am the first,
I am the last,
I am the beginning,
And also the end,
I am the smoke
I am the gas,
I am the bullets,
I am solid
But I am also vapor,

I am nothing
Yet I am everything

I am the Holocaust

– Unknown

We Will Not Forget

You must not forget,
Don't let the sands of time erase.
Their bloodstained hands, our days of fear,
Don't let our memory disappear,

Here's our vow that we remember,
That no matter what the pain,
We'll give our pledge to tell the story
That your lives were not in vain.

We will not forget,
Won't let the sands of time erase.
Their bloodstained hands, your days of fear,
Won't let your memory disappear.

We will not forget,
The unlived lives,
What might have been.
As time goes by from year to year,
Won't let your memory disappear.

Don't let the memory disappear.

– Ellen Hubert and **Sharon Lands Shepherd**

Student Quotes of the Paper Clip Project

"*The project made me see life in a whole new perspective. I view people no different than how I view myself. I respect everyone despite different religious views or race. We may be different, but in reality we are all the same.*"

–Madison Gamble

"*This project instilled in me an others-first mindset. My life would be wasted if all I ever did was serve myself, and that is why I choose to focus on the needs of others. It also taught me not to fear those who are different from me, but instead, to learn from, love and respect them. Diversity is a wonderful thing and should be welcomed everywhere. These lessons have changed my life and helped shape me into the advocate that I am today.*"

–Hannah Underwood Pratt

Paper Clips and Butterflies

At the foot of Whitwell Mountain
a coal-mining town endures.
The mines left; the people stayed.
Raised their children—
Going to church on Sunday morning—
In this poverty-stricken place.

One day the children learned of a Holocaust,
a desire to understand gave them purpose. A goal.
They'd collect paper clips, a symbol for every soul
 like the Norwegians did.

A compassionate world showed up.
Six million. Then, eleven. Then, thirty million!
A railcar as a resting place.
Butterflies gathered with the children
to mourn
to remember
to celebrate
those not extinguished after all.

– Sharon Shadrick

Linda Hooper's Reflections

Recently I was asked why anyone would want to read about a project that began twenty-five years ago. My answer: because today the project still stands as an example of how to overcome racism and prejudice.

For more than two decades—and carrying into the future—the work of the students at Whitwell Middle School and the Whitwell community lit the way to fight increasing anti-Semitism. Our young people lead tours of the Children's Holocaust Memorial for visitors from all over the world. They are involved in a project called A Book By Me. With this project Whitwell Middle School students are interviewing survivors and veterans who witnessed the horrors of the Holocaust to write and illustrate their stories. Beginning in fifth grade, our students read literature about the Holocaust and other human rights tragedies. Each student is encouraged to develop a service project that will make the community better.

As I look at our world today, I see a lack of respect for others is rampant. Some of our country's leaders and aspiring leaders seem bent on destroying the reputation of anyone who opposes their opinion. We all seem to be so caught up in social media and broadcasting every thought entering our head that we have lost the power to listen to and respect the opinions of others. People, hiding behind the media, use violence and disrespect as their chosen means of communication. Cooperation, community, love of our fellow man almost seem to be foreign concepts.

Enter *Paper Clips*, a reminder that vision and personal involvement can accomplish more than time spent involving only a person's thumbs. This is a story that demonstrates how even the smallest symbol, the poorest community, and people with no visible power can create a memorial to make a powerful statement for the world. It is a message that must never be forgotten. This book is written to remind everyone that all it takes is ONE person, idea, community with a vision to change the world and give hope for a better tomorrow.

As I look back, there are no words that adequately describe my feelings toward all the people involved in the making of the Children's Holocaust Memorial and the documentary *Paper Clips*. Bob Johnson's Johnson Group provided the crew to film and edit *Paper Clips* without any assurance that it would be profitable. Joe Fab and Julia Eddy spent hundreds of hours viewing the footage of *Paper Clips* and editing the 180 hours of film down to the eighty-three-minute version. Elliot Berlin and the film crew—including "Sully" Sullivan, the audio engineer in charge of sound; Amy Jones; and camera man Michael Marton—treated the story, the students, the staff, and the community with love and respect. Alison Krauss and Charlie Barnett's beautiful rendition of "Jubilee" captured so poignantly the heart of the project and the suffering of the victims of the Holocaust. Matthew Hiltzik provided the expertise to get the film produced, into theaters, and accepted by the public. Survivors shared their hearts, their stories, and their artifacts with us. The people in our town gave their hearts, time, and talents to the memorial. Sandra Roberts began teaching the first group of students and parents without pay. David Smith brought the internet study by the iEARN Foundation to our attention. Peter and Dagmar Schroeder located the railcar in Robel, Germany, secured the funding to purchase the car, and made the arrangements to transport it to the United States. The Roberts, Higdon, and Powell families worked diligently on the grounds surrounding the car and the celebration event. CSX Transportation brought the car to Chattanooga. Fletcher Trucking provided the transportation from Chattanooga to Whitwell Middle School. B & B Crane Company set the car up at its new home. Barras Lebovitz used the occasion of his Bar Mitzvah to raise funds to have the car moved when the new Whitwell School was built. The Hassons, Janice B. Levy, and Darrell Fine made the trips to South Africa possible for our students. Bob Cusick sponsored a trip for our students to go to all the major concentration camps in Poland. Kathryn and Alan Greenberg established a scholarship fund for our students. My husband and my family supported this project in every way possible. Alison Lebovitz, with the help of Joyce Tatum and Grant Knowles, created the One Clip at a Time curriculum, bringing the message of the project to educators all over the world. It would take a thousand pages to give adequate recognition to the students, staff, community members, and people from all over the world who have made this project the beacon of hope it is today.

– Linda M. Hooper

The Woman and Philosophy Behind the Paper Clips Project

In her decades as an educator, Linda Hooper has formulated core beliefs about how students are best enabled to learn and grow. She has imparted these beliefs to the many teachers she has inspired and to parents and public officials who have influence over schools.

1. Students should be given the opportunity to express their creativity and imagination.
2. Learning can be best acquired through an emphasis on experience and problem solving.
3. Learning can be fun and enjoyable.
4. Educators should continually search for new ideas that will make the classroom more fun, enjoyable, and interesting to their students.

These core beliefs developed from the deep foundations built by her life experience. She has written, "My core beliefs come from the understanding that every child has unique, innate abilities. These abilities should be enhanced by the child's home, family, school staff, and adults with whom they interact.

"The reality is that children do not all have equal starts in life. Homes can be unstable. Poverty keeps children from an environment that is rich in opportunities to learn. For a hungry child, learning will not be a top priority.

"Children are not prefabricated pieces of society that can be shoved into a predetermined mold. They are humans. Each one has marvelous talents to make our future brighter. Neither their place in society nor that of their educators, parents, or community should be judged by standardized testing that does not relate to their uniqueness.

"Public schools serve all children, both those blessed with opportunities and those ignored and left with little or no foundation for educational success.

"Government leaders, school administrators, school staff, parents, and community members must all come to the table to develop methods to ensure that all students experience success—success that provides for their social, mental health, and academic needs.

"The best educators are the ones who see each child as an individual with hopes, dreams, fears, and needs. These educators are constantly seeking resources to meet the needs of all children. They must be supported by their communities and have opportunities to grow through adequate paid time for advanced learning and interacting with other successful educators to develop the best instructional methods.

"Education does not occur in a vacuum. It takes hard work, commitment, and the realization that only through cooperative efforts will every child achieve their optimum level."

Linda is known for being able to pack a verbal punch. She gets to the heart of matters in sayings known as "Lindaisms." People who know her will smile and nod at the list assembled here.

1. Common sense is the rarest commodity on the face of the earth.
2. Everything on the earth is a unique creation of God.
3. To disrespect another person is to disrespect God.
3. No person is perfect.
4. All people make choices every day.

5. Those choices show us the person's character.
6. If we are to have a world where peace, respect, and love are the rule and not the exception, it is up to each individual to work to make that happen.
7. Everyone makes mistakes. Not everyone learns from them. Those who do become better, stronger people.
8. Life is what you make of it.
9. Every action we take, every word we speak has an impact on our world.
10. The influence of cell phones and social media is causing a serious breakdown in honest communication.
11. Testing students constantly causes stress for all, as do pre-set curriculums that don't consider the uniqueness of each student.
12. The best learning occurs by doing.
13. If you see an issue that needs to be addressed, don't just complain, go do something to change it.
14. Spend twice as long listening as you do speaking.
15. Always look at people when speaking to them.
16. Nothing in my Bible says I must like everybody, but it does say I have to love them.
17. Is what you say and do something you would be proud to have written on your tombstone to be remembered by people all over the world?
18. We must always look for ways to involve students in projects that will make them concerned, compassionate citizens.

Beyond the Railcar

There's a treasure tucked away down in the valley
Just hop on 28—then take it straight till you find God
And what happens there is much more than a movie
It's the story of a town that's gone beyond…

The Philly Friends embarked upon a mission
To get on a plane and make their way to Whitwell, Tennessee
And it turned into an annual tradition
It's the story of a town that's gone beyond…

Beyond the railcar, there's a sacred love and friendship
From Big John's pick and shovel in the middle of town to the hat
*   of William Penn*
Beyond the railcar, there's a commitment to our future
And together we all pledge never again
And together we all pray never again

As we gather and light candles as one family
Remembering and honoring the millions who were lost
But our friendship and our love is a reminder
Of the blessing that our hallowed paths have crossed

Beyond the railcar, there's a sacred love and friendship
From Big John's pick and shovel in the middle of town to the hat
*   of William Penn*
Beyond the railcar, there's a commitment to our future
And Together we all pledge never again
And together we all pray never again

(*Instrumental*)

We stand arm and arm and heart to heart so strong
And lift our voices high so the whole world can hear this song

Beyond the railcar, there's a sacred love and friendship
From Big John's pick and shovel in the middle of town to the hat
     of William Penn
Beyond the railcar, there's a commitment to our future
And together we all pledge never again

Beyond the railcar, there's a sacred love and friendship
From Big John's pick and shovel in the middle of town to the hat
     of William Penn
Beyond the railcar, there's a commitment to our future
Together we will stay forever friends
Together we will stay forever friends

– Lyrics by **Norman Einhorn,**
    music by **Cantor Harold Messinger**

Resources

Babcock, Stephen. "Their Voices Unite Against Hatred: Youngsters from Tennessee Remember the Holocaust." *The* (Quincy, MA) *Patriot Ledger*, April 10, 2006.

Condra, Casey. Interview by Sharon Shadrick. September 17, 2019.

Cusick, Bob. Interview by Sharon Shadrick. September 10, 2019.

Einhorn, Norman. Interview by Sharon Shadrick. November 7, 2021.

Floyd, Morgan. Interview by Sharon Shadrick. September 21, 2020.

Frazier, Jenny. "In Her Own Words: A Trip to South Africa." *South Pittsburg Hustler*, August 31, 2006.

Gamble, Madison. Interview by Sharon Shadrick. September 27, 2020.

Higdon, Gregory. Interview by Sharon Shadrick. October 11, 2020.

Higdon, Mary Jane. Interview by Sharon Shadrick. January 9, 2020.

Hiltzik, Matthew. Interview by Linda Hooper and Sharon Shadrick. September 15, 2019.

Hudson, Karsen. Interview by Sharon Shadrick. May 27, 2020.

Karpfen, Michael. Letter to Whitwell Middle School. May 21, 2001.

King, Brett. "Greenberg Awards Whitwell Middle with $500,000." *Jasper* (TN) *Journal*, December 20, 2005.

Lebovitz, Alison. Interview by Linda Hooper and Sharon Shadrick. September 22, 2019.

Long, Kayla. Interview by Sharon Shadrick. April 15, 2022.

Malsy, Emily Hooper. Interview by Sharon Shadrick. September 6, 2019.

McDaniel, Taylor. Interview by Sharon Shadrick. April 10, 2020.

One Clip at a Time (website). Accessed March 20, 2024. https://oneclipatatime.org/.

Payne, Roger. Interview by Sharon Shadrick. October 6, 2020.

Perkel, Andrew. Letter to Linda Hooper. n.d.

Pratt, Hannah Underwood. Interview by Sharon Shadrick. October 26, 2020.

Roberts, Sandra. Interview by Sharon Shadrick. July 2, 2019.

Rudoren, Jodi. "Holocaust Told in One Word, 6 Million Times." *The New York Times*, January 26, 2014. https://www.nytimes.com/2014/01/26/world/middleeast/holocaust-told-in-one-word-6-million-times.html.

Slatton, Dalton. Interview by Sharon Shadrick. December 30, 2019.

Schroeder, Peter W., and Dagmar Schroeder-Hildebrand. "The Car Is Found." *Six Million Paper Clips*. Minneapolis, MN: Kar-Ben Publishing, 2004.

Shadrick, Drew. Interview by Sharon Shadrick. June 8, 2020.

Smith, David. Interview by Sharon Shadrick. July 26, 2019.

Smith, Dita. "A Measure of Hope." *Washington Post*, April 7, 2001.

Storch, Bernard. Letter to Linda Hooper and Whitwell Middle School students. May 30, 2001.

White, Grace Hooper. Interview by Sharon Shadrick. February 4, 2020.

Zagnoev, Jennie. Interview by Sharon Shadrick. February 1, 2021.

Zhong, Stephanie. Interview by Sharon Shadrick. October 18, 2020.

Acknowledgments

SHARON SHADRICK

Special thanks to all the Whitwell Middle School students (past and present), WMS staff, and Whitwell community members who provided interviews for the book: Casey Condra, Dalton Slatton, Drew Shadrick, Emily Hooper Malsy, Grace White, Gregory Higdon, Karsen Hudson, Kayla Long, Morgan Floyd, Roger Payne, and Taylor McDaniel.

Thank you to Alison Lebovitz for your interview and ongoing work with One Clip at a Time.

Thank you to Matthew Hiltzik, Bob Cusick, and Norman Einhorn for your heartfelt interviews and dedication to the project.

Thank you to the original Holocaust study group teachers, Sandra Roberts and David Smith, for being the catalyst for this project. Thank you to Taylor McDaniel for carrying it forward.

Many thanks to Mary Jane Higdon for her interview and sharing her photographs with us.

Thank you to Stephanie Zhong and Jennie Zagnoev for your interviews.

Thank you to the positive letter writers: Michael Karpfen, Andrew Perkel, and Bernard Storch.

A special thank you to my writing friends, Sara Thomas Pierce, Natalie Jenkins Kimbell, Chrissie Anderson Peters,

Sharon Waters, and the Honey Badgers and Rules Schmoolz writing groups. Thank you to my writing teachers, Darnell Arnoult, Denton Loving, and Diane Zinna.

Thank you to my developmental editor Nora Gaskin Esthimer of Lystra Books and my copy editor and book designer Kelly Lojk. Your encouragement throughout the final stretch kept me going.

Thank you, Linda Hooper, for this once-in-a-lifetime privilege to tell this story.

More than anything, thank you to my husband, Mark Shadrick, and my children, Amanda Elliott, Hannah Shadrick Hummel, and Steven Casey Shadrick, who were always in my corner.

Sharon Shadrick, left, and Linda Hooper

About the Authors

SHARON SHADRICK is a full-time writer after retiring from twenty years of teaching English and writing labs in Tennessee schools. One of her proudest accomplishments as a teacher was running an after-school program for young writers in which she helped them get published in local publications. Her poems have been published in the Women of Appalachia Project's *Women Speak Anthology*, Volume Nine; *Pine Mountain Sand & Gravel: Appalachian Fusion*; and *The Mildred Haun Review*. She is currently working on her memoir. She lives in Dunlap, Tennessee, with her husband, two grandchildren, and three rescue dogs.

LINDA HOOPER is the retired principal of Whitwell Middle School and co-founder of the Children's Holocaust Memorial. She worked in public education for over thirty years. Linda is active in her church, leading youth on missions and food drives for foreign countries. Currently, as chairperson of the Whitwell Education & Heritage Center, Linda is leading the effort to provide adequate facilities for the Orena Humphreys Public Library, the Miner's Museum, the Veterans Center, the Senior Citizen's Center and the library, archives, and artifacts collection of the Children's Holocaust Memorial. Linda resides in Whitwell with her husband of sixty years, Edward Hooper, a retired pharmacist. They have two children and five grandchildren.